T0208589

Praise for *Alternatives to Capitalism*

"This is an extraordinary book. At one level it is a profoundly informed discussion of critical issues of radical systemic structure. At another it is a model of how a thoughtful dialogue on challenging and highly contested issues should be carried on. A must read for anyone seriously interested in how to conceive the possible forms of fundamental systemic change."

Gar Alperovitz

"If you've ever wondered what a democratic economy could really look like, treat yourself to this engaging (and wonderfully comradely) conversation about two leading schools of contemporary socialist thinking—participatory economics and real utopias—by their distinguished founders."

Juliet Schor

"Although the failings of neoliberalism are increasingly clear—social, economic and environmental—the myth of 'no alternative' remains a powerful one. In this book, Robin Hahnel and Erik Olin Wright debate what an alternative might look like. Should it involve markets? Is a role for markets compatible with democratic values? To be so, what other institutions and policies must be in place? Their discussion is a superb introduction to these fundamental debates."

Stuart White

Alternatives to Capitalism

Proposals for a Democratic Economy

ROBIN HAHNEL

ERIK OLIN WRIGHT

VERSO

London • New York

First published by Verso 2016
© Robin Hahnel and Erik Olin Wright 2016
First published as an ebook by New Left Project 2014

The moral rights of the authors have been asserted

1 3 5 7 9 10 8 6 4 2

Verso
UK: 6 Meard Street, London W1F 0EG
US: 20 Jay Street, Suite 1010, Brooklyn, NY 11201
versobooks.com

Verso is the imprint of New Left Books

ISBN-13: 978-1-78478-504-8
ISBN-13: 978-1-78478-506-2 (US EBK)
ISBN-13: 978-1-78478-505-5 (UK EBK)

British Library Cataloguing in Publication Data
A catalogue record for this book is available from the British Library

Library of Congress Cataloging-in-Publication Data
A catalog record for this book is available from the Library of Congress

Typeset in Sabon by Hewer Text UK Ltd, Edinburgh
Printed in the US by Penguin Random House

Contents

A Dialogue

Ed Lewis

Poverty, exploitation, instability, hierarchy, subordination, environmental exhaustion, radical inequalities of wealth and power—it is not difficult to list capitalism's myriad injustices. But is there a preferable and workable alternative? What would a viable free and democratic society look like?

Alternatives to Capitalism: Proposals for a Democratic Economy presents a debate between two such possibilities: Robin Hahnel's "participatory economics" and Erik Olin Wright's "real utopian" socialism. It is a detailed and rewarding discussion that illuminates a range of issues and dilemmas of crucial importance to any serious effort to build a better world.

Is it worth devoting energy to thinking about alternatives to capitalism? There is a tradition within anti-capitalist politics that thinks not. It is argued that idle speculation distracts from what really matters: the struggles emerging in the here and now, which are the soil from which any emancipatory future will spring. Moreover, if participation in those struggles is done on the basis of a preconceived vision, their creativity and experimentation may be inhibited.

However, a compelling case can be made that serious visionary work can invigorate and strengthen radical politics. The most powerful movements of the left in the twentieth century failed to produce a desirable alternative to capitalism, leading instead to authoritarian "really existing socialism" in the USSR and its satellites, on the one hand, and "humanized capitalism" of social democracy, on the other. This has led to pessimism about widespread transcending capitalism, even among radical movements and their sympathisers. By contrast, a left animated by a shared vision, resting on the kind of credible intellectual foundations that Robin and Erik supply, could help provide confidence and strategic direction that lacking to day.

This dialogue brings together two writers who, motivated by such considerations, have devoted substantial efforts to thinking systematically about a next economic system. Both Robin and Erik began this process in the 1990s, when the collapse of the USSR heralded a new era of capitalist triumphalism. Robin and his collaborator Michael Albert built on ideas that had emerged within the libertarian socialist tradition in the twentieth century—including council communists, anarcho-syndicalists and elements of the New Left—to develop a plausible anti-capitalist economic model known as "participatory economics." This model dispenses with the defining features of a capitalist economy—private ownership, markets and a hierarchical division of labor—replacing them with self-managing worker and consumer councils, and a novel procedure of participatory planning. His latest book on the subject is *Of the People, By the People: The Case for a Participatory Economy* (AK Press, 2012), where he presents a comprehensive, yet accessible explanation of the model.

In the 1990s Erik initiated the Real Utopias Project, editing a series of books canvassing and assessing a range of proposals for emancipatory institutional arrangements. This eventually led to the publication of his own work, *Envisioning Real Utopias* (Verso, 2010). By far the most ambitious book in the series, developed in part through a speaking tour of 18 countries over four years, it outlines a novel conception of socialism, anchored in the concept of "social empowerment"; a variety of general institutional configurations that could facilitate its realization; and a detailed discussion of strategy for social transformation.

In *Alternatives to Capitalism* Erik and Robin bring to bear the ideas developed in *Of the People, By the People* and *Envisioning Real Utopias*. Part one focuses on participatory economics, while part two focuses on real utopian socialism. Each part opens with a lead essay that summarizes the main ideas of the author's approach, followed by a critical commentary by the other author, followed by a rejoinder. The distinctive nature of this text is the depth of the dialogue that emerges. New arguments and ideas surface in each of the six contributions, while key issues are revisited throughout and subjected to sustained evaluation. The result is a work that, even as it covers a range of issues in economics, social theory and history, achieves a rare degree of depth and thoroughness.

Important points of disagreement emerge. These concern, among other things, the level of detail to which post-capitalist visions should aspire, the future of markets, and whether a revolutionary strategy has a credible role to play in anti-capitalist politics. Readers will have to make their own judgments about the competing arguments on these issues—a task made easier by the constructive spirit with which Erik and Robin pursue their disagreements, with no time wasted on straw-manning or point scoring. This reflects the genuine political desire, shared by the authors and publishers, that motivates *Alternatives to Capitalism*: to strengthen the intellectual resources of anti-capitalist politics. We hope it makes a worthwhile contribution to this most vital of tasks.

PART ONE

CHAPTER I

The Case for Participatory Economics

Robin Hahnel

Curious Jane: "So, if you don't like capitalism, what do you want instead?"

Modern anti-capitalist: "Certainly not old-style bureaucratic Communism!"

Curious Jane: "Fine . . . But then what DO you want?"

Modern anti-capitalist: "I want an economic system that promotes economic democracy, economic justice, and human solidarity, without sacrificing economic efficiency."

Curious Jane: "Who wouldn't! . . . But people sometimes mean different things when they use these words. Can you be more specific?"

Supporter of participatory economics: "Yes I can—and you are quite correct to demand clarification, because often disagreements over how best to organize the economic system stem from different conceptions of what these words mean. By economic democracy, I mean having decision making power in proportion to the degree one is affected by a decision. By economic justice, I mean economic reward commensurate with sacrifice, or effort. By human solidarity, I mean having concern for the wellbeing of others. And by economic efficiency, I mean using scarce productive resources where they are most socially beneficial and not wasting people's hard work."

Curious Jane: "That is all well and good . . . I'm not sure I agree entirely with your definitions, but let's suppose for now that I did. Exactly how would you organize the economy to achieve these goals?"

The model of a participatory economy—which I briefly summarize below—is an answer to Jane's last question. It is *not* an answer to other important questions, such as: In the short run, what can we do in the here and now to best promote the above goals? Or, in the long run, what strategy might maximize our chances of making a successful transition from the economics of competition and greed to an economics of equitable cooperation? These are important, but quite different questions. Participatory economics is simply a coherent description of how a fully developed system of equitable cooperation could function. It is not a transition strategy or political program.

A Participatory Economy[1]

The major institutions "we"[2] propose to achieve economic democracy, economic justice, and human solidarity while protecting the environment and ensuring efficiency are: (1) self-governing democratic councils of workers and consumers where each member has one vote, (2) jobs balanced for empowerment and desirability by the members of worker councils themselves, (3) compensation according to effort as judged by one's workmates, and (4) a participatory planning procedure in which councils and federations of workers and consumers propose and revise their own interrelated activities without central planners or markets, under rules designed to generate outcomes that are efficient, equitable, and environmentally sustainable.

Over the past twenty years some critics have disagreed with our goals while others have objected to one or another of our recommendations for how to achieve them. Erik has offered his own evaluation of participatory economics on pages 252–65 of *Envisioning Real Utopias*.[3] In my reading Erik seems to agree with our goals—although, as one would expect, his formulation and argument differ in some regards. Most importantly, and unlike many who have criticised

---

1   The "model" of a participatory economy briefly presented here was initially developed jointly by myself and Michael Albert in the 1990s, and is now often referred to as "Parecon." I do not use this acronym because I believe it conveys an otherworldly impression and fosters a cultish mentality I find detrimental to advancing discussions like this one among people thinking seriously about economic system change.

2   When I say "we" I mean not only myself and Michael Albert, but also a growing network of people around the world who, without necessarily agreeing on every detail, nonetheless refer to the participatory economic "model" as the kind of alternative to capitalism they favor. In short, "we" includes all of us who answer Jane's question by explaining how a participatory economy could work. As should be expected, "we" do *not* always agree about short-run programs or long-run transition strategies for getting there!

3   Erik Olin Wright, *Envisioning Real Utopias* (London and New York: Verso, 2010).

participatory economics, Erik seems to share our views about what economic justice and economic democracy mean and require.

Unless I am mistaken, Erik is also supportive of compensation based on effort and trying to balance jobs for desirability and empowerment, although he worries it may prove difficult to achieve these goals. To be specific, we propose that each worker council come up with its own procedures for assigning what we call "effort ratings" to one another, which become the basis for their members' consumption rights in neighborhood consumption councils. We call this an effort-rating committee, but its composition and procedures are left up to each council, and we fully expect different worker councils to come up with very different ways to go about this. In particular, compensation is not something that can be negotiated when new members are hired by worker councils in a participatory economy. Everyone is free to apply for membership in any worker council of her choice, and worker councils are free to hire whomever they wish from their applicant pools— subject to strict rules outlawing discrimination of course. However, since remuneration is determined only after someone has worked, and is to be based only on differences in efforts, or sacrifices, as judged by co-workers, the hiring decision is completely separate from decisions about compensation levels in a participatory economy.

While some market socialists do not favor self-management with one-worker/one-vote, Erik agrees with most advocates for market socialism who see worker self-management as one of its major virtues.[4] However, to ensure that formally equal rights to participate in decision making in one's workplace translate into truly equal opportunities to participate, supporters of participatory economics propose that in addition to one-worker/one-vote, jobs within

---

4   The first model of market socialism developed by Oskar Lange and Abba Lerner in the 1930s proposed that enterprise managers be appointed by the state, not chosen by a self-governing worker council where every member has one vote. In the 1990s, John Roemer proposed a different variant of "managerial market socialism" in which workers also were not "sovereign" over their own workplace. However, the majority of market socialists have historically supported worker self-management. Jaroslav Vanek and Branko Horvat proposed models of "worker self-managed market socialism" in the 1960s. David Schweickart and Michael Howard have proposed slightly different versions of worker self-managed market socialism in the past twenty years. Erik strongly supports a "worker self-managed" rather than a "managerial" version of market socialism.

workplaces be balanced for empowerment. We argue that as long as some workers sweep floors all day, every day, while others attend meetings of various kinds all day, every day, formally equal rights to participate at worker council meetings will not translate into truly equal opportunities to influence firm decisions. Again, we refer to a job-balancing committee and discuss how it might function, but leave particulars up to individual worker councils, and expect wide variations in how they would try to combine tasks in job descriptions so that everyone's work experience contains some empowering tasks, and pleasant and unpleasant tasks are shared by all. Unlike many other market socialists who object to job balancing as inefficient and an infringement on individual economic freedoms, Erik seems to agree with us that these objections are not compelling, and that achieving meaningful economic democracy requires job balancing.

Which means that while many other market socialists object to our proposals for how to reward work and organize the production process, the major area of disagreement between Erik and supporters of participatory economics has to do with the best way to coordinate the interrelated activities of different worker councils and consumers—or what economists call the economy's "allocative mechanism."

What Is Participatory Planning?

Erik's principal objection to the "model" of a participatory economy is the proposal to replace markets with a procedure we call "participatory planning." Here the distinction between a long-run goal and a transition strategy is crucial. I have never been under the illusion that we can replace markets with participatory planning immediately. The market system has been growing and deepening for hundreds of years, and regrettably still has the allegiance of an overwhelming majority of the population. Since the "system change" we seek is highly democratic it can only happen when we have convinced a significant majority to support replacing the market system with participatory planning. Therefore, I personally have long argued that while the market system persists, much of our transition strategy necessarily consists of various ways to "socialize" markets—as Erik and other proponents of market socialism put it—in order to ameliorate their detrimental effects. This is why I believe supporters of participatory economics can work together with market socialists on many campaigns to "tame" markets in the here and now. In other words, in my view the difference is not that market socialists fight to tame markets while proponents of participatory economics do not. The difference is that advocates of participatory economics fight to tame markets *until a majority supports replacing them altogether with something far better*, while market socialists fight to tame markets *to keep them*.

The case for eventually replacing markets altogether logically has two parts: (1) Demonstrating how and why markets—even if "tamed"—would still have undesirable consequences. (2) Demonstrating that there is an alternative way to coordinate a productive division of labor that is both feasible and less problematic. I can postpone the first part of this "case against markets" until after Erik presents his reasons for believing that eliminating markets entirely is unnecessary and undesirable. Here I confine myself to the second part—the "how and wherefores" of the participatory planning alternative. To keep things simple I will confine myself to the annual participatory planning procedure, taking care to correct some common misconceptions.

The Planning Procedure

The annual participatory planning procedure takes place in the context of an investment plan that has already decided what investment goods will be produced this year and how they will be distributed to increase capacities of different industries at year's end. It also takes place when the stocks of all kinds of natural capital (e.g., acres of fertile land), produced capital (e.g., lathes), and human capital (e.g., people-hours of welding labor) available for use during the year are known.[5] What the annual planning procedure "decides" is which worker councils will use which productive resources, what those worker councils will use their primary and intermediate inputs to produce, how intermediate goods produced will be distributed among worker councils, and how consumption goods produced will be distributed among consumer councils and federations. In other words, the procedure yields what economists call a comprehensive, annual production-consumption plan.

---

5   In other words, the "demand" for each investment good to be produced this year, and the "supply" of every input that cannot be produced this year are "givens" when annual planning begins.

Only worker councils, consumer councils and federations participate in the annual planning procedure. Each worker and consumer
council, and each federation of consumer councils participates by
submitting a proposal for what that council or federation wants to
do, i.e. councils and federations make what we call "self-activity
proposals." There is a single "iteration facilitation board" (IFB) that
performs one very simple function. The IFB announces current estimates of the opportunity costs of using each kind of "capital"—
natural, produced, and human—the social cost of producing every
produced good and service, and the damage caused by every pollutant. The IFB raises its estimate of the "indicative price" for anything
in excess demand in the previous round of the planning procedure,
and lowers its price for anything in excess supply, after which councils
and federations revise and resubmit new "self-activity" proposals
until a feasible plan is reached, i.e. until there is no longer excess
demand for any natural resource, any kind of physical capital, any
category of labor, any intermediate or final good or service, or any
pollutant.[6]

---

6 Note: A great deal of what has been written about the need for
supercomputers and modern information technologies for a participatory
economy to work is simply wrong. For example, the IFB does not need a powerful
computer at all. It merely adds up and compares the demand and supply for each
natural resource; each category of labor; each final, intermediate, and capital
good or service; and each pollutant. In terms of "technology" the IFB might want
an abacus but has no need for a supercomputer! Nor do actors in the planning
procedure need to do anything other than multiply quantities by "indicative
prices" and add them up to calculate the estimated social costs of consumption
requests and the social benefit to cost ratios of production proposals. Again,
nothing requiring fancy computer capabilities.

Assuming central planners could obtain accurate, detailed information about
the capabilities of all production units, in order to be efficient, central planning
does require supercomputers capable of solving very large mathematical
programming problems—which, incidentally, have been available for decades
now. However, this is not the case for participatory planning. Nobody in a
participatory economy needs to acquire detailed information about the
production capabilities of production units, and nobody requires the services of
supercomputers. Where relatively new modern technology would be helpful in
running a participatory economy is in adjusting for changes during the year from
what was planned and approved. Computerized inventory management systems
and "real time" supply chains—which are now fixtures in the global economy—
make adjustments during the year much smoother than they would have been a
few decades ago.

Individual workers participate only within their own worker council, helping formulate and revise their own worker-council proposal. Individual consumers participate only within their own neighborhood consumer council, (1) voting for delegates to higher-level consumer federations responsible for requesting higher-level public goods, (2) making their own and approving the individual consumption requests of others, and (3) deciding on requests for neighborhood public goods. The process whereby individual consumption requests are approved is internal to each neighborhood consumption council, and not part of the participatory planning procedure itself. The process whereby federations of consumer councils decide what higher-level public goods to ask for is also up to them, and not part of the planning procedure.

Each round in this social, iterative procedure begins with new, more accurate estimates of opportunity and social costs, followed by revised proposals from all councils and federations in light of new information about how their desires affect others. Each council and federation must revise and resubmit its own proposal until it meets with approval from the other councils. Consumption council and federation proposals are evaluated by multiplying the quantity of every good or service requested by the estimated social cost of producing a unit of the good or service, to be compared to the average effort rating of the members of the consumption council or federation requesting the goods and services. If, for example, the average effort rating for a neighborhood consumption council is equal to the social average, this should entitle them to consume goods and services whose production costs society an amount equal to the average cost of providing a neighborhood consumption request. A neighborhood council with higher than average effort ratings (indicating that they had made greater than average sacrifices as workers) is presumably entitled to a consumption bundle that costs society more than the average; a neighborhood council with lower than average effort ratings should presumably only be entitled to a consumption bundle that costs less than the average.

The estimates of opportunity and social costs generated during the planning procedure make it easy to calculate the social cost of consumption requests. This is important information for councils and federations making consumption requests since otherwise they have no way of knowing the extent to which they are asking others to bear burdens on their behalf. It is also important for councils and federations which must vote to approve or disapprove consumption requests of others, since otherwise they have no way of knowing if a request is fair (consistent with sacrifices those making the request have made) or unfair (in excess of sacrifices made).

Production proposals are evaluated by comparing the estimated social benefits of outputs to the estimated social costs of inputs. In any round of the planning procedure the social benefits of a production proposal are calculated simply by multiplying quantities of proposed outputs by their "indicative" prices—including negative prices for proposed emissions of pollutants—and summing. The social costs of a production proposal are calculated by multiplying inputs requested by their "indicative" prices and summing. If the social benefits exceed the social costs—that is, if the *social benefit to cost ratio* of a production proposal exceeds one— everyone else is presumably made better off by allowing the worker council to do what they have proposed. On the other hand, if the social benefit to cost ratio is less than one, the rest of society would presumably be worse off if the workers go ahead and do what they have proposed, unless there is something "the numbers" fail to capture. Again, the "indicative" prices make it easy to calculate the social benefit to cost ratio for any production proposal, allowing worker councils making proposals to determine if their own proposals are socially responsible, and giving all councils who must vote to approve or disapprove production proposals of others an easy way to assess whether or not those proposals are socially responsible.

This procedure "whittles" overly ambitious proposals submitted by worker and consumer councils about what they would like to do down to a "feasible" plan where everything someone is expecting to be able to use will actually be available. Consumers requesting more than their effort ratings and allowances warrant are forced to either reduce the amounts they request, or shift their requests to less socially costly items if they expect to win the approval of other councils who have no reason to approve consumption requests whose social costs are not justified by the sacrifices of those making them. Similarly, worker councils are forced to either increase their efforts, shift toward producing a more desirable mix of outputs, or shift to a less costly mix of inputs, to win approval for their proposals from other councils who have no reason to approve production proposals whose social costs exceed their social benefits. Efficiency is promoted as consumers and workers attempt to shift their proposals in response to updated information about opportunity and social costs in order to avoid reductions in consumption or increases in work effort. Equity is promoted when further shifting is insufficient to win approval from fellow consumers and workers, which can eventually only be achieved through consumption reduction or greater work effort. As iterations proceed, consumption and production proposals move closer to mutual feasibility, and estimates more closely approximate true opportunity and social costs as the procedure generates equity and efficiency simultaneously.

Because estimates of opportunity and social costs are available to all it is easy for anyone to calculate whether or not a consumption or production proposal is socially responsible. This means there is no need for a central planner to be the final arbiter, approving or disapproving proposals. Councils can vote "yea" or "nay" on other councils' proposals without time-consuming evaluations or contentious meetings, except in occasional cases requiring special review.

There are important technical issues of concern to economists. In this regard it has been demonstrated that the participatory procedure outlined above will eventually reach a feasible plan that is a Pareto optimum under less restrictive assumptions about technologies and preferences than those necessary to prove that the general equilibrium of a private enterprise, market economy will do so. In particular, participatory planning accommodates externalities and public goods efficiently, and generates reasonably accurate estimates of damages from pollution whereas market economies do not.[7] But this is what it boils down to:

---

7 Readers interested in these technical issues should see Michael Albert and Robin Hahnel, Chapter 5 in *The Political Economy of Participatory Economics* (New Jersey: Princeton University Press, 1991); "Socialism as It Was Always Meant to Be," *Review of Radical Political Economics* 24, no. 3–4 (Fall and Winter 1992): 46–66; "Participatory Planning," *Science and Society* 56, no. 1 (Spring 1992): 39–59; and Hahnel, "Wanted: A Pollution Damage Revealing Mechanism," forthcoming in the *Review of Radical Political Economics*.

When worker councils make proposals they are asking permission to use particular parts of the productive resources that belong to everyone. In effect, their proposals say: "If the rest of you, with whom we are engaged in a cooperative division of labor, agree to allow us to use productive resources belonging to all of us as inputs, then we promise to deliver the following goods and services as outputs for others to use." When consumer councils make proposals, they are asking permission to consume goods and services whose production entails social costs. In effect, their proposals say: "We believe the effort ratings we received from co-workers indicate that we deserve the right to consume goods and services whose production entails an equivalent level of social costs."

The planning procedure is designed to make it clear when a worker council production proposal is inefficient and when a consumption council proposal is unfair, and allows other worker and consumer councils to deny approval for proposals when they seem to be inefficient or unfair. But initial self-activity proposals, and all revisions of proposals, are entirely up to each worker and consumer council itself. In other words, if a worker council production proposal or neighborhood council consumption proposal is not approved, the council that made the proposal—nobody else—can revise its proposal for resubmission in the next round of the planning procedure. This aspect of the participatory planning procedure distinguishes it from all other planning models, which advocates believe is crucial if workers and consumers are to enjoy meaningful self-management.

CHAPTER 2

Participatory Economics: A Sympathetic Critique

Erik Olin Wright

Let me begin, like Robin did in his opening contribution to this dialogue, by affirming a very broad range of issues on which we are in deep agreement:[1]

Strong egalitarianism is a core value. We both adopt a radical egalitarian understanding of social justice, although we use slightly different language to express our views. A just system of economic distribution is one that combines an unconditional guarantee of income, sufficient to provide for (generously interpreted) basic needs, with additional income that is proportionate to some broadly understood notion of effort or sacrifice. Robin refers to the first of these conditions as a condition for a *humane* economy, not a just economy, and treats only the second condition as a matter of justice, whereas I feel it is unjust to deny people equal access to the material means necessary to live a flourishing life. But this makes no practical difference in our views about what constitutes a desirable system of distribution.[2] We both reject inequalities in material conditions of life that are the result of talents or contributions or brute luck and certainly of power.

---

1 My analysis here is based more on Robin's book, *Of the People, By the People: The Case for a Participatory Economy*, rather than simply his initial contribution to this dialogue.

2 Using the term "justice" in a more restrictive way only really matters if one also believes that considerations of justice always trump other values. Some liberal political theorists seem to argue this—that whenever there is a conflict of values between justice and something else, justice decides; it has, to use the philosophers' term, "lexical priority." Neither Robin nor I give justice that kind of over-riding weight. In Robin's terms it is just as important that a society be humane as just, and in places in his analysis he is willing to accept as a legitimate trade-off some departures from justice in the name of efficiency (see my discussion below of the problem of innovation).

The quality of work, not just the material rewards from work, is an issue in justice. Robin expresses this concern in his principle of "balancing jobs"—the idea that all jobs, to the extent possible, should contain the same mix of tedious and enjoyable tasks, pleasant and unpleasant activities, routine and "empowered" responsibilities. As an ideal, all jobs should be equally desirable from the point of view of whatever qualities people value within work. This is a complex regulative ideal, and while in practice it will never be fully realized, deviations are a matter of injustice. People in jobs that, for pragmatic reasons, have more burdens in this sense (i.e. a less desirable balance of tasks) should thus be compensated with greater income or more leisure or in some other appropriate way.

Radical, substantively meaningful democracy. Democracy, if taken seriously, means that people should be able to meaningfully participate in making decisions over things that affect their lives. Robin correctly argues that the full realization of that principle means that the weight of individuals' preferences in decisions should be roughly proportional to how much any given decision affects them. This is obviously a very complex idea to put into practice in a fine-grained way, and any practical implementation will at best be a rough approximation of the ideal itself. This conception of democracy provides grounding for the kind of nested system of participatory decision-making bodies that is at the heart of the institutional design of Robin's model.

Capitalism has destructive effects on all of these values. Finally, we both argue that capitalism systematically contradicts the realization of all of these values, and while it is sometimes possible to mitigate some of the deficits with various kinds of public policies within capitalism, transcending capitalism is a necessary condition for the fullest possible realization of democratic-egalitarian values.

That is a lot of agreement. Where we differ is in our views of certain important aspects of the institutional design of an alternative that is best suited to realize these common values.

Robin feels very confident that a complex, large-scale, well-functioning economic system—in principle even a global economy—could exist in which markets have been completely replaced by participatory planning. While he acknowledges that the actual design of economic institutions in a post-capitalist participatory economy will evolve through experimentation and democratic deliberation, he nevertheless argues that the goal should be the complete elimination of markets, and his hypothesis is that such an economy would function in ways that would be robustly sustainable. Sustainability, in the context of a democratic-egalitarian economy, means that the institutional configuration in question would be continually endorsed by the broad majority of participants in the economy since they have the power to change the rules of the game if they don't like the way things are working. There will inevitably be trade-offs across the different values that a participatory economy hopes to realize. A particular set of institutional rules of the game is a way of navigating those trade-offs. A stable system is one in which the continual over-time results of the operation of the system reinforce the actors' commitment to those rules. Robin's hypothesis, then, is that a participatory economy in which markets play no role would be sustainable in this sense.

My position is that the optimal institutional configuration of a democratic-egalitarian economy is much more likely to be a mix of diverse forms of participatory planning, state regulatory mechanisms, and markets. I, like Robin, am disposed to give great weight to the participatory mechanisms because of the ways these embody values of equality and democracy, but I am very skeptical that these could ever completely displace markets, or even, really, that this should be some bottom-line goal to which we aspire. I want a robustly and sustainably democratic-egalitarian economy, but my expectation is that the institutional designs *that people in such an economy would actually choose* (through experimentation and learning) will include a significant role for markets. This is a *prediction* rather than a *prescription*. I do not know what institutional configuration of different forms of economic organization would work best, nor what, in practice, the trade-offs will be between different configurations. What I predict, then, is that a configuration in which markets play no role would not be sustainable in the sense I am describing.[3]

---

3 Contrary to what some people argue, sustainability of a post-capitalist democratic-egalitarian economic system of the sort proposed by Robin would not require that it generate high rates of economic growth (unless, of course, it were also the case that the participants within such an economy would be sufficiently dissatisfied with the rates of growth—or non-growth—that an alternative was seen as preferable). What sustainability requires is that the participants' commitment to the institutions is not undermined by the effects of its operation.

I also believe—as I will argue in more detail later—that this expectation may not be so different from what Robin's model would, in practice, generate iteratively over time. Robin acknowledges that the actual functioning of his model for a participatory economy combines initial rounds of planning (through his nested participatory councils of various sorts) and after-the-fact, continual "adjustments" that occur for a variety of reasons. Depending on the scale of processes through which these adjustments occur and exactly how they are executed, they could function a lot like markets. And since this is an ongoing process in which the adjustments in one period constitute inputs for subsequent planning, it is not so clear that the marketish processes would play only a peripheral role.

This way of thinking about the issues implies that the concept of "markets" is not a binary. In a binary conception of markets you either have markets or you don't; any given transaction is either a market transaction or it is not. A non-binary conception recognizes that exchanges can be heavily regulated and affected by collective priorities, but still involve things being bought and sold in which the prices are affected by supply and demand as well as regulatory constraints. Such exchanges involve significant market and non-market mechanisms. Or to take a different kind of example, in my usage of the term "markets," garage sales (and their internet equivalents like Craigslist) are a form of market relations: items are put up for sale; the prices tend to be higher in the morning than at the end of the day in response to the demand by consumers for the things on offer; more garage sales are likely to occur (i.e. the supply of goods for sale through this mechanism will be greater) in an economic environment where there are lots of people who like to buy used things. A participatory economy, I would predict, is likely to allow, perhaps even encourage, things like garage sales. Of course capitalism is not like a garage sale writ large because the power relations implicated in capitalist markets are vastly different from those in a neighborhood garage sale. Garage sales are a very minor aspect of the market system in contemporary capitalism. But nevertheless, they constitute a particular form of market processes.

In what follows I focus on five elements of Robin's model:[4]

---

4   Throughout this paper I will address my comments strictly to Robin's writing on participatory economics. I recognize, of course, that many of the ideas were developed jointly with Michael Albert.

household consumption planning; the mechanisms for dealing with externalities; public goods planning; risk-taking innovation; the organization of work and pay. My skepticism is greatest about the first of these, so I will spend the most time exploring its mechanisms and ramifications. For the others I have specific issues to discuss, but I broadly endorse what I see as the core principles they each attempt to achieve.

Participatory Planning of Household Consumption
In his book (p. 115), Robin describes four basic principles that his model of participatory planning is meant to embody, all of which are touched on in his opening contribution to this dialogue as well:

1. We want people to have input in decisions to the degree they are affected.
2. We want outcomes to be fair and efficient.
3. We want procedures to promote rather than undermine solidarity.
4. We want all our plans to be environmentally sustainable.

These are all desirable principles. What I wish to interrogate is the second element in the second criterion: efficiency.[5] Specifically, I am skeptical that an institutional design in which markets have been completely eliminated—where they play no role whatsoever in economic coordination—is likely to be as efficient as an institutional configuration that combines a variety of forms of economic coordination: participatory planning, centralized regulations, and market interactions. I will not argue for the superiority of markets over participatory planning; I am arguing for the desirability of an institutional ecosystem of the economy that combines a variety of institutional forms and mechanisms.

---

5 Like Robin, I reject the narrow meaning of efficiency adopted by many economists as the profit-maximizing use of resources in a market. Rather, efficiency refers to the allocation of all resources (including the time of all participants) that best reflects the optimal trade-offs for alternative uses of those resources. Efficiency must include a full account of positive and negative externalities.

I will focus first on the aspect of the planning process which I feel is the most problematic, the planning of household consumption. The planning of consumption is in many ways the pivotal process within the participatory economy model for this is what most fundamentally dictates what is produced in the economy. As Robin writes:

> There is complete freedom of choice in a participatory economy regarding what one wishes to consume. Moreover, consumer preferences determine what will be produced in a participatory economy whereas they only do so very imperfectly in market economies. Since markets bias consumer choice by overcharging for goods whose production or consumption entail positive external effects, undercharging for goods with negative external effects, and over supplying private goods relative to public goods, markets influence what will be produced in systematic ways that deviate from consumers' true preferences. Participatory planning is carefully designed to eliminate these biases which both infringe on 'consumer sovereignty' and generate inefficiencies. (p. 80)

Robin's model of the participatory planning of public goods—collective consumption in its various forms—does not pose the same problems. By their very nature, public goods are always planned in one way or another, and Robin's proposed model of participatory planning of public goods in which councils at the appropriate scale for a given public good are the primary site for deliberation over public goods seems absolutely right. I also have much less to say about the various forms of production planning—annual plans, long-term investments and development planning. These are certainly important, and some of what I have to say would be relevant to those arenas of planning as well, but I also think that the weight of the participatory planning elements for those kinds of decisions would, in an optimal social design, be much greater than for household consumption planning.

One final provisional comment: I am not sure that in all details I fully understand the operation of the participatory planning mechanisms that are at the core of Robin's model. I have read Robin's opening contribution and the relevant chapters in the book numerous times, as well as Michael Albert's book *Parecon: Life After Capitalism* and a few other discussions of these issues, but nevertheless there are parts of the exposition that, for me anyway, remain unclear. I have not been able to develop an intuitive understanding of how all of this actually works, how all of the pieces fit together, and especially why the proposed institutional design eliminates all perverse incentives so that everyone provides perfect information to everyone else, thus making the system invulnerable to opportunism by individuals or groups.[6]

Let me begin by reviewing the basic elements, as I understand them, of the way consumption planning for individual households takes place in Robin's model. This process is covered to some extent in Robin's opening contribution but there it is interwoven with an account of production planning as well. For my purposes it is useful to distil the consumption planning process, which I take to be as follows:

1. At the beginning of the process the IFB, announces current estimates of indicative prices for everything (consumption items, inputs to production, labor, etc.) based on estimates of opportunity costs and positive and negative externalities in the production of all goods and services.

2. Each household begins the process with a budget constraint determined by: (a) an effort rating based on the contributions of labor effort by all household members during the previous year, (b) a level of consumption allowances for people excused from participation in production (children, elderly, severely disabled, etc.), and (c) a consumption allowance for people who simply don't want to work (this is, in effect, an

---

6 I don't think my lack of intuition here is because I have not read the technical economic papers that Robin refers to in his essay, papers which he describes as proving that his planning mechanism generates optimal outcomes. I am not skeptical that the mathematical models that are elaborated in those papers show these things. What I am skeptical about is that the mathematical models can adequately represent the way these institutions would actually function over time. I suppose this is in part the skepticism of a sociologist about the empirical robustness of conclusions that can be drawn from formal mathematical models of complex social processes.

unconditional basic income, presumably set at a level to fully meet basic needs).

3. Every year individual households submit to their neighborhood consumer councils their requests for all the things they anticipate consuming in the following year, given the household budget constraints. In effect, they pre-order their annual household consumption.

4. The powers of neighborhood consumption councils with respect to household consumption include: authorizing borrowing and saving of households; approving their consumption requests; discussing and proposing neighborhood public goods. The household proposals are reviewed by neighborhood consumption councils. If they fall within the budget constraint of the household, then they would normally be approved automatically. If there is a request for consumption above this level—in effect a request for a loan—this would normally be reviewed more closely. If the proposals are rejected, households revise them.

5. Neighborhood consumption councils aggregate the approved individual consumption requests of all households in the neighborhood, append requests for whatever neighborhood public goods they want, and submit the total list as the neighborhood consumption council's request in the planning process.

6. Higher-level federations of consumption councils make requests for whatever public goods are consumed by their membership.

7. On the basis of all of the consumption proposals along with the production proposals from worker councils, the IFB recalculates the indicative prices and, where necessary, sends proposals back to the relevant councils for revision.

8. This iterative process continues until no revisions are needed.

There are two issues that I would like to raise with this account about how household consumption planning would actually work in practice: (1) How useful is household consumption planning? (2) How marketish are "adjustments"?

How Useful Is Household Consumption Planning?

Robin argues that this planning process would not be especially demanding on people. In his words:

> We are well aware that consumers will misestimate what they ask for and need to make changes during the year, and that some consumers will prove more reliable and others more fickle. As a matter of fact, being quite lazy about such matters, I would not bother to update my consumption proposal at all! And being very irresponsible about communication I would also, in all likelihood, fail to respond to the prompt from my neighborhood consumption council reminding me to send in a new proposal for the coming year. I would simply allow my neighborhood council to re-enter what their records show I actually ended up consuming last year as my pre-order again for this year. Sound difficult?
>
> The easiest way to think about this is to imagine each consumer with a swipe card that records what they consume during the year as they pick it up, and compares their rate of consumption for items against the amount they had asked for. If one's rate of consumption for an item deviates by say 20 percent from the rate implied by the annual request, consumers could be "prompted" and asked if they want to make a change. If at the end of the year the total social cost of someone's actual consumption differs from the social cost of what they had asked, and been approved for, they would simply be credited or debited appropriately in their savings account. (pp. 86–7)

Here is one of the things I don't understand about this process as described: A key issue for any meaningful planning process is the classification of the items in the consumption bundle. When a consumer submits a plan, how fine-grained are these categories? For example, is "clothing" a category, or is the relevant category "shirts," or "dress shirts," or "highly tailored dress shirts" or "highly tailored silk dress shirts"? Among food items, is "jam" a category, or is "imported French blueberry jam" a category? For something like "books", is it enough to estimate how much I plan to spend on books in a year, or do I have to know which titles I am likely to buy? Also: if I travel, then my consumption of certain things will extend far beyond the boundaries of my immediate location. If I estimate how much of the value of my consumption will be in restaurants, does it matter that some of these might be in Paris or New York rather than in the city where my neighborhood consumption council is located? I can certainly imagine making gross estimates of very large categories of consumption—like clothing or travel or food—but not of fine-grained items.

The problem is that the gross categories provide virtually no useful information for the actual producers of the things I will consume. It does not help shirt-makers very much to know, based on the aggregation of individual household consumption proposals, that consumers plan to spend a certain percent of their budget on clothing; they need to have some idea of how many shirts and of what style and quality to produce since these have very different indicative prices (and thus reflect different opportunity costs and positive and negative externalities). But consumers can hardly be expected to have a reasonable idea of their consumption for the future at that level of detail—how many cheap versus expensive meals I will consume in what cities, etc. Robin does not explain how detailed the consumption list is expected to be, whether it is built on categories like "food" or the list needs to be broken down into "wild-caught smoked salmon" and "gourmet organic chunky peanut butter." In some places he seems to suggest that the categories will be quite coarse-grained, as in the above quotation when he writes: "If one's rate of consumption for an item deviates by say 20 percent from the rate implied by the annual request, consumers could be 'prompted' and asked if they want to make a change." That prompting would make sense for a broad category like clothing, but not a detailed specification like "silk neckties".

Since the coarse categories would not be useful for planning by federations of worker councils, and this is the fundamental purpose for pre-ordering consumption, I will assume that the finest level of detail is required. This would involve for any complex economy hundreds of millions of items—basically, all of the differentiated final consumption items around which producers make decisions about how much to produce. Since it is beyond the ability of people to meaningfully specify such an inventory a year in advance, the solution, of course, is for households to simply use the list of specific items they actually consumed from the previous year. This seems to be what Robin suggests that he, and probably most people, would do: "I would simply allow my neighborhood council to re-enter what their records show I actually ended up consuming last year as my pre-order again for this year." (p. 86) If overwhelmingly this is what people would do, then there is actually no real need for them to submit pre-ordered consumption "proposals" at all since the total consumption of specific items from the previous year is already known to producers—this equals the total of all the goods and services produced that were acquired by consumers. The plans for production for the future, then, in effect would be done pretty much as they are done now: producers would examine the sales[7] and trends of sales in the recent past, and make their best estimate of what to produce for the next year on that basis. Indeed, since producers and their sector federations can continually and efficiently monitor these trends, they are in a position to make updates to plans in an ongoing way on the basis of the actual behavior of consumers, rather than mainly organize their planning activities around annual plans animated by uninformative household pre-orders.

There is a certain irony here. Robin argues in favor of pre-ordering by saying:

A participatory economy is a planned economy. This means we must have some idea what people want to consume in order to formulate a plan for how to produce it. In market economies consumers do not "pre-order," and instead producers are left to guess what consumers will eventually demand . . . the convenience for consumers of never having to pre-order in market economies is actually bought at the expense of a significant amount of economic inefficiency as resources are wasted producing more of some goods and less of others than it turns out people want. (p. 84)

But if pre-ordering is really a fiction since most people will behave as Robin predicts that he will behave, then it will still be the case that "producers are left to guess what consumers will

---

7 I use the term "sales" here for convenience since, strictly speaking, in Robin's model of participatory economics the nature of the exchange between consumer and worker is not exactly buying and selling in the usual market sense.

eventually demand." Of course, in a participatory economy where there is little competition among producers and they are organized into federations of worker councils, it will be easier for them to get full and detailed ongoing data on consumer choices relevant to their ongoing plans, so their guesses are likely to be more accurate than in capitalism. But what is gained by having households submit a formal pre-order of a year's worth of consumption, given how they are likely to behave, instead of having the producers simply use all of the relevant data from actual patterns of consumption in their sectors as the basis for estimating what will be consumed in the next year?

There is one other secondary issue I'd like to raise about household consumption planning and neighborhood consumer councils. I understand—and support—the role of neighborhood councils in planning neighborhood public goods. I don't understand why my personal consumption should be the business of a neighborhood council, even apart from the problem already discussed of the usefulness of the procedures involved. The general principle underlying participatory planning is that people should be involved in decisions *to the extent it affects them*. But why does my personal consumption have any effect whatsoever on my immediate neighbors any more than it does on anyone else? They are affected by the division of consumption between public goods and private consumption, but not by the content of what I consume, so why should they have any role in that at all? The same goes for my requests for loans or credit: why is this the business of my neighbors?

How Marketish Are "Adjustments"?
In his opening piece in this dialogue, Robin only sketches part of the planning process—the annual plan as generated by worker and consumer councils. However, in his book he acknowledges that the initial annual plans will only be approximations and that throughout the year adjustments will have to be made. With respect to household consumption, Robin affirms the value of consumers being able to consume what they want in a participatory economy: "There is complete freedom of choice in a participatory economy regarding *what* one wishes to consume" (p.80). This means that the pre-ordered household consumption plans will result in lots of deviations, and

accordingly, lots of adjustments. Here is how Robin foresees these adjustments taking place:

> One of the functions of consumer councils and federations is to coordinate changes in consumption among themselves. If another consumer wants more of an item I pre-ordered but no longer want, there is no need to change the amount the agreed upon production plan called for. Whenever consumer councils and federations (which will function like clearing houses for adjustments) discover that changes do not cancel out, the national consumer federation will have to discuss adjustments with industry federations of worker councils. Computerized inventory management systems and "real time" supply chains are already fixtures in the global economy, which makes adjustments much smoother than they would have been only a few decades ago. (p. 85)

The actual process by which these adjustments will occur is not very clear to me, but even with the best inventory management systems one can imagine, there will still be excess inventory of some goods in the system and shortfalls in others. The most obvious way that excess inventory will be dealt with is by allowing people to acquire these things less expensively. To use conventional language, where there is excess supply, prices will be reduced, whether on an erratic basis or as "end of season sales." To be sure, this means that the prices of these goods will be not reflect the opportunity costs of their initial production or the positive and negative externalities that were taken into consideration in determining their initial "price." But it will reflect the opportunity costs consumers face in deciding to acquire one good or another.

There will also be shortages in goods. In some specific situations, this is inherent in the nature of the goods. For a theater performance there is a difference between the best seats and the worst seats in the house, although the production costs of the "seat" in terms of material inputs, and positive and negative externalities, don't differ across seats. For other goods, especially some novel good, there will be shortages just because of the time it takes to produce as much as people want. One way of dealing with shortages in the supply of something is rationing, for example through a lottery. People could buy a theater ticket and be randomly assigned a seat. Or they could order a new product and the length of time they had to wait until they received it could be randomized. That is one perfectly good solution and satisfies a certain interpretation of equality. Or access could be based on a first-come-first-served basis, with the accompanying night-long vigils to get tickets when a box office opens. But one could also charge people more for the items that are in short supply. If this occurs in a social context of effort rating–based income—that is, a system in which everyone has the same choice of how much income they want to earn by simply deciding how much effort they want to expend—then charging more for goods in short supply simply means that those people who really want the good more will be able to choose to consume it sooner. In Robin's model, the extra income generated by these higher-than-cost-of-production prices would not go into the pockets of the producers. Their incomes would continue to be based on their own effort expenditure. All that would change is that consumers would be able to decide whether it was sufficiently important for them to have the good in question sooner that they would be willing to consume less of something else or work harder for some period of time.

This description of how adjustments to annual consumption plans would work looks a lot like certain critical aspects of markets: prices adjust to disequilibria of supply and demand. This, of course, does not render the economy overall a "free market economy". The fact that the costs of externalities, positive and negative, are built into the base price of goods, is not something that happens in market systems, and certainly the fact that purchasing power is based on effort-expenditures is not derived from a market mechanism. Yet, allowing the actual prices consumers face to be systematically affected by supply and demand is a market process. And depending upon the actual, practical degree of adjustment needed in the system, this could generate significant varia-tion in prices. My prediction is that in a participatory economy, the participants would decide that this was often a reasonable way of deal-ing with the problem of discrepancies between supply and demand.

Public Goods Planning

My concerns about participatory planning of public goods are much less than about household consumption. Public goods do need to be discussed and decided on by public bodies, and it is certainly desirable as much as possible to have the deliberation over public goods be by the circles of people who will actually benefit from them. For many, perhaps most public goods, the appropriate level for such decision-making will be at a fairly macro level—cities and regions and even higher levels. But there certainly are some important public goods where the key domain of collective consumption is the neighborhood, and it is appropriate that the people directly affected have the major role in deciding the details on these. This is what, in a limited way, participatory budgeting of municipal infrastructure investments tries to do. Robin's model of participatory planning of public goods can be thought of as a radical extension of some of the elements of participatory budgeting. I strongly endorse the general spirit of the idea that public goods planning should be maximally participatory at whatever geographical level is most relevant for a particular kind of public good.

The participatory decision-making over collective public goods consumption, however, does not require consumer councils that also approve or disapprove individual household consumption plans. What a neighborhood public goods council needs to decide is the division between public and private consumption within the neighborhood (i.e. how much of income that would otherwise go to households should be allocated to those public goods) and what specific public goods to produce. There is no inherent reason why this needs to be connected to approval of plans for what households consume privately. For this reason, I think it would be better to call these public goods councils than consumption councils.[8]

Unlike the planning for household consumption, public goods planning at whatever level it occurs requires real public deliberation: meetings, debates, bargaining, formulation of plans for specific projects, etc. Participatory planning of public goods—at the neighborhood level and beyond—will be a critical feature of a post-capitalist, democratic-egalitarian economy, especially because it is likely

---

8　If these councils are also meant to deal with the problem of negotiating pollution prices, then this could be treated as the planning of "public bads" consumption. The mandate for these councils would thus revolve around the dual task of planning both public goods and public bads.

that the balance between private and public consumption will shift considerably in the public direction. Planning such public goods in a deeply democratic way, however, will be arduous, not simple, because it is unlikely there will be a smooth consensus over the balance between household consumption and public goods or over the specific mix of public goods. This will raise the Oscar Wilde problem of socialism taking up too many evenings, but it is worth it.

There is one set of issues around public goods planning in Robin's model that was not clear to me: the role of Government institutions rather than just consumer federations. On one interpretation of Robin's participatory economics model, virtually all government functions are replaced by consumer councils and federations and by worker councils and federations. There might still be a role for government around certain kinds of rule making and rule enforcing—for example, things like speed limits or enforcing the accurate reporting of pollution discharges so the planning process (however it is organized) has accurate information with which to deal with externalities. But the government would have no responsibility for planning and producing any kind of public goods.

There may be reasons, however, to make a distinction between the way public goods are connected to people as *consumers* and public goods that are linked to their status as *citizens*. For one thing, some public goods do not fall neatly into the distinction between consumers and producers. Educational public goods, for example, serve people's needs both as producers and consumers, and the same can be said for health care. Public transportation systems are public goods for people both as consumers and producers. Democratically accountable government institutions might be more appropriate than consumer or producer federations for providing these kinds of multi-dimensional public goods and monitoring their performance. But it is also the case that there is a range of public goods (or aspects of public goods) which, in certain important ways, serve the needs of people neither as consumers or producers but as members of a community. Public gathering places are public goods, and in a sense they are "consumed" by people when they gather for public purposes, but this is only one aspect of their social meaning. They also contribute to constructing a public sphere and public identities. Public spaces for performing music and theater are a public good in which these activities are consumed by audiences and produced by performers; but they are also sites for the collective project of affirming cultural identities and purposes. Aspects of the mass media are like this as well insofar as the media contribute to civic mindedness and solidarities.

Perhaps these kinds of civic public goods would be adequately attended to by nested councils and federations organized around consumption. But perhaps not. It may be that they would be better fostered by citizens' assemblies organized as political bodies within a federated state structure. As a sociologist I am somewhat skeptical that a system of councils organized around the social role of people-as-consumers and institutionally embedded in a planning process concerned with negotiations with workers' federations through the intermediation of the IFB's management of indicative prices is the optimal setting for deliberations over civic public goods.

The Problem of Externalities

One of the most important elements in Robin's critique of markets is their inability to adequately take account of negative and positive externalities of production on their own. If there were no negative and positive externalities, and if there were no concentrations of power in markets (and thus no monopoly rents), then the equilibrium prices of goods in markets would be unlikely to differ dramatically from those generated by participatory planning. Both systems would produce prices closely in line with the total real costs of production.[9] But of course, there are substantial positive and negative externalities. Among the most interesting and original parts of the model of participatory economics is the way Robin proposes to deal with these issues.

The key problem for any planning process with respect to externalities is figuring out a way to assign quantitative values to externalities so that these can be adequately reflected in the prices of the things that people consume. Assigning a value to such costs and benefits involves two steps. First, there is a technical problem of identifying

---

9 The mix of public goods and private goods would, of course, be likely to be very different under any system of democratic planning.

the inventory of actual negative and positive side-effects of a given production process. This is the work of scientists and technical experts. For example, environmental negative externalities, involve identifying the amounts of different pollutants generated in a given production process, and scientifically showing what the ill-effects of given levels are. Producers, of course, should be required to report these levels, and this generally requires some kind of monitoring and enforcement mechanism, but these levels only have meaning in a planning process when there is a way of assessing the harms they cause. This is where science plays a pivotal role: providing information about such things as the increase in risk of cancer caused by a given level of a particular pollutant.

This brings us to the second step: figuring out the value to be placed on the harm. It would always be possible, of course, to declare that zero pollution is the only acceptable level. This could, however, turn out to be enormously costly in many situations, and thus some device needs to be concocted to put a value on the harms caused by a given level of pollution compared to the costs of reducing the pollution. This is where Robin's model has a particularly original suggestion. Basically he proposes that federations of consumer councils at the appropriate geographical level in which an environmental negative externality of production is present be allowed to decide on the level of compensation they need in order to be willing to accept a given amount of pollution. This is like saying: I'll be happy to have a cancer risk increase by 10 percent if you increase my consumption by 20 percent. Here is how the process works:

> In each iteration in the annual planning procedure there is an "indicative price" for every pollutant in every region impacted representing the current estimate of the damage, or social cost of releasing a unit of that pollutant into the region. What is a pollutant and what is not is decided by federations representing those who live in a region, who are advised by scientists employed in R&D operations run by their federation[10] . . . If a worker council

---

10 This particular detail—that the federation corresponding to a region affected by pollution have its own R&D department employing scientists—does not seem like a workable institutional design for the technical issues involved in

proposes to emit x units of a particular pollutant into an affected region they are 'charged' the indicative price for releasing that pollutant in the region times x . . . The consumer federation for the region affected looks at the indicative price for a unit of any pollutant that impacts the region and decides how many units it wishes to allow to be emitted. *The federation can decide they do not wish to permit any units of a pollutant to be emitted, in which case no worker council operating in the region will be allowed to emit any of that pollutant. But, if the federation decides to allow x units of a pollutant to be emitted in the region, then the regional federation is 'credited' with x times the indicative price for that pollutant.*

What does it mean for a consumer federation to be "credited?" It means the federation will be permitted to buy more public goods for its members to consume than would otherwise be possible given the effort ratings of its members. Or, it means the members of the federation will be able to consume more individually than their effort ratings from work would otherwise warrant. (pp. 124–5)

If the consumers harmed by pollution are unwilling to permit, at the level of compensation offered by the price of pollution, as much pollution as the producers would like, then the price for units of pollution will go up in the next round of the iterative planning process. And if the price is too high, then the federation of consumers affected by pollution will want to purchase more units of pollution than the producers will want to emit, and so the price will decline in the next round. This continues iteratively until an equilibrium is reached.

This is indeed a clever device. The principal alternative discussed by Robin is pollution taxes (called "Pigouvian taxes") set equal to the value of the negative externalities and imposed on polluters. The

---

assessing environmental externalities. The boundaries of regions impacted by given pollutants will vary enormously. Some will be smaller than cities, some much larger regions. It does not seem necessary that consumer federation in each region have its own R&D department and hire its own scientists. It is not clear to me why, for these kinds of technical regulatory matters, state institutions with field offices and extension services wouldn't do this job more effectively.

problem with such taxes, as Robin points out, is the difficulty in knowing how high to set the taxes to fully cover the amount of damage caused by the pollution. What Robin proposes is a specific method for determining the level of those taxes by organizing what is very much like a series of collective auctions for the right to pollute. The auctions continue until there is an equilibrium between the demand for pollution payments and the supply of pollutants offered by producers. Robin sees the process as iterative adjustments in the indicative price for pollution, but it could equally well be described as a method for determining the Pigouvian taxes on pollutants. This looks a lot like a quasi-market in which the buyers and sellers are councils of various sorts acting as agents for individuals as consumers and workers.

This device for calculating the value of externalities could work well in some situations. But it could easily become extremely complex and cumbersome. There are a number of issues in play: The geographical boundaries of a particular source of pollution may or may not correspond to the boundaries of existing consumer federations. If the smallest scale federation that includes all of the affected areas is the relevant decision-making body, then this would often include large numbers of consumers unaffected by the pollution. This undermines the sense in which the valuation of damage by the federation as a whole would reflect the subjective valuation of those most affected by the pollution in question. Would coalitions of most affected consumers be able to constitute themselves as an ad hoc federation and insist on higher prices for the rights to pollute? Furthermore, even apart from the fact that different parts of a region will have differential damage, there may be considerable heterogeneity among the population of an area with respect to how much they care about the damage in question. This is obviously a problem in any system for constructing a metric of damage from pollution, but it adds special complexity when the process is meant to be participatory and deliberative. Would consumers with stronger anti-pollution preferences be able to form an ad hoc federation to demand higher pollution prices? Could they constitute a blocking coalition?

Finally, unless I am misunderstanding the process involved, the procedures Robin advocates would likely generate considerable heterogeneity in the pollution taxes (i.e. the negative externality charges built into "indicative prices") faced by producers of similar goods in different places. This means producers in areas where consumers don't care so much about pollution would be able to produce at lower cost. However, there is no restriction (as far as I can tell) that they only distribute their products to the pollution-indifferent consumers. This means that the same goods will be available to consumers elsewhere at lower and higher indicative prices depending on the pollution preferences of consumers in the places where production takes place. This begins to look like a situation that generates market pressures on the high cost producers.

Given that there are many thousands of potential pollutants, and the geographical damage-boundaries of different pollutants from the same production process will often be different, the actual process by which negative externalities are dealt with through iterated annual planning by consumer federations could become extremely cumbersome and inconsistent. In such a situation, consumers might decide that they prefer a simpler system that combines government regulations that impose various kinds of limits on allowable pollution with a system of uniform taxes on different types of environmental externalities. Given that, in a participatory economy, the democratic accountability of government policy making will not be distorted by concentrations of private power as in capitalism, consumers-as-citizens might prefer the uniformity and predictability of such a regulatory system even though it would be less immediately responsive to the particular preferences for levels of pollution of citizens-as-consumers.

Risk-Taking Innovation

I have no problem with the broad principle that a great deal of investment in new projects—perhaps even a large majority of investments—could be effectively organized through some kind of participatory, democratic planning process involving various kinds of councils and federations. Whether this would be precisely organized along the lines of worker councils and sectoral federations as proposed by Robin or through some other institutional arrangement is a secondary matter; the important point is that it is plausible that much investment can be productively allocated through directly democratic processes.

What is less clear to me is whether the optimal system would eliminate all features of more market-like allocations for at least some investments. Is there good reason to believe that the optimal system would allow no investments outside of the decision-making processes of councils and federations? Consider the following example:

Suppose a group of people have an idea for some new product but they cannot convince the relevant council or federation to provide them the needed capital equipment and raw materials to produce it. There is just too much skepticism about the viability of the project. An alternative way of funding the project could be through a form of crowdsourcing finance along the lines of Kickstarter. The workers involved would post a description of the project online and explain their specific needs for material inputs. They appeal to people (in their role of consumers) to allocate part of their annual consumption allowances to the project. Consumers might decide, for example, to put in extra hours at work in order to acquire the extra funds needed for their contribution, or they might just decide to consume less of some discretionary part of their consumption bundle. Once sufficient funds are raised in this manner, the project can proceed. Such a device could be used for an experimental theater project that the relevant sector federation (which would in effect function like an arts council) thinks is a waste of resources. Or it could be used for some new manufactured product.

There are a variety of motivations that might lead people to voluntarily make this allocation. They might believe in the social value of the project and therefore be willing to give the funds as an outright grant. This is currently the motivation behind a range of Kickstarter projects in the arts. Or they might be really keen on the product, and give the funds in exchange for a promise of being the first to get the product itself at an equal value to what they gave. This would, in effect, be simply a long-term pre-order of the product, although operating outside of the mechanism of the IFB. But potential contributors to the project might also only be interested in contributing if they got a positive return on their "investment". This would look much closer to market investment.

The question, then, is should such practices be prohibited in a participatory economy? Especially if a positive return on crowdsourced investments is allowed, these projects would constitute a kind of quasi-market niche in the participatory economy. Robin argues that new worker councils should be prohibited from raising capital outside of the planning process. Here is what he says about new start-up worker councils:

> In a participatory economy new worker councils bid for the resources they need to get started in the participatory planning process. If they submit a proposal that is accepted, they're good to go. Otherwise not . . . But just as banks judge the 'credibility' of new entrepreneur's business plans in capitalism, industry federations judge whether or not a group who has proposed to form a new worker council are 'credible.' (pp. 111–2)

Mostly, I suppose, industry federations will make sound judgments. After all, they have no incentives to block creative, well-thought-out proposals. But they may be excessively risk averse and be subject to other kinds of biases. And, of course, there could be factions, in-groups and out-groups, and other forms of social exclusion that marginalize some kinds of projects. Certainly around artistic endeavors this is likely to happen periodically. In Robin's model if a group of workers fail to get permission from a federation, they are out of luck (this is how I interpret the expression "otherwise not" in the above quotation).[11]

I think more flexibility than this is likely to be desirable. One thing, I think, would be pretty certain: if such processes are allowed, a fair number of projects outside of the ordinary planning process are likely to emerge, and this potentially could generate undesirable

---

[11]   It is worth noting that in capitalism there is a very wide range of ways that small businesses can acquire the necessary capital for projects: There are ordinary banks, of course, but in many countries there are a wide variety of specialized banks with different criteria for making loans, including some with social and environmental mandates. Community banks are different from national banks, and state banks are different from multinational banks. There are also government agencies in many countries that give far below market-rate loans for targeted purposes and even outright grants. And there are things like Kickstarter and other unconventional ways of raising capital. I am not at all saying that this generates a fair and open access to capital. It does not in capitalism. The point is that this constitutes a heterogeneous institutional environment. I think a participatory economy is also likely to function best with qualitatively distinct devices for funding projects.

inegalitarian dynamics. Clearly a set of rules would have to be in place to counteract such forces. They could take the form of strict caps on the amount of extra income that could be generated as returns on such "private" investments as well as on the income generated by the projects for the workers. There could be rules by which once the viability of an investment project is demonstrated, it had to gradually fold into the ordinary annual planning model for future inputs. The firms created through these outside-of-planning processes could still be required to be internally governed democratically. And of course they would be subjected to the same externalities taxes (or their functional equivalent) like any other productive activity.

My prediction is that in a vigorously democratic participatory economy, the participants themselves would be likely to endorse a space for something like unplanned risk-taking of this sort. People would come to recognize certain kinds of rigidities and blind spots that occur whenever all projects need to seek permission from formally constituted collective bodies, and that a looser, more free-wheeling alternative could make the system as a whole more dynamic. While this means that there will be modest deviations from the purest model of participatory planning and effort-based remuneration, my prediction is that most people will see this as worthwhile. Under the background conditions of strong equality of material conditions and democratic control over the rules of the game, a certain amount of capitalism between consenting adults might be seen as a good thing.

This prediction, of course could be wrong. It could turn out that the corrosive effects on egalitarian norms of allowing even modest forms of market-like investments would be seen as so unpalatable that an absolute prohibition of such practices might be the democratic decision after a period of experimentation. But I think this is unlikely. The optimal economic "ecosystem" for a democratic egalitarian economy, I predict, would probably have something like participatory democratic planning processes as the dominant mechanism for allocating investments, but this would be combined with a variety of other economic allocation processes, including some with a strong market character.

Even though my specific views on this matter differ from Robin's, in other places in his analysis Robin acknowledges that in a real participatory economy people might well decide, democratically, to deviate from the core principles of the system in order to solve certain incentive problems. In discussing the problem of dynamic efficiency, for example, Robin carefully explores the problem of the incentives for innovation. He asks, about innovation:

> since innovations are shared with all immediately [because there are no patent protections], where is the incentive for individual worker councils to innovate rather than wait for special R&D units or other worker councils to do so? In particular, will it prove desirable to provide material rewards to innovating workplaces, above and beyond what their members' sacrifices entitle them to? (p. 108)

He answers as follows:

> There is good reason to believe in an economy where it is unlikely that status will be achieved through conspicuous consumption, and where social serviceability will be more highly esteemed, that rewarding workers in highly innovative enterprises with consumption rights in excess of sacrifices may not be necessary. *However, if people in a participatory economy come to the conclusion that extra rewards for workers in innovating enterprises are needed, any such rewards will be determined democratically by all citizens.* (p. 109, emphasis added)

I agree completely with this formulation. It affirms the idea democratic choice over the rules-of-the-game is the decisive principle at work in a participatory economy. In this case, if there is a trade-off between strict adherence to the remuneration according to effort principle and dynamic efficiency, then it is reasonable for citizens to decide to allow some inequality in income to emerge. In effect, this means, they would be willing to allow some injustice in the income mechanisms in exchange for improvements in the rate of innovation. I am making the same point with respect to planning and an investment market.

The Organization of Work and Pay

In terms of the underlying normative principles, I fully support the central ideas of Robin's framework for both the organization of work and for pay: balanced job complexes and pay determined by effort rather than contribution. Where I would like to raise some issues is with the practical implementation of the ideals.

Balanced Jobs

In my book, *Envisioning Real Utopias*, I define the equality principle of justice this way: "In a just society, all people have equal access to the social and material conditions necessary to live a flourishing life." This is entirely in keeping with Robin's proposal for the organization of work in terms of "balanced jobs". One of the social conditions for a flourishing life is meaningful and interesting work, and the idea of equal access to those conditions of work means that the work of all members of a workplace should have relatively equal mixes of tasks with positive and negative attributes (e.g., tedious and enjoyable tasks, stressful and relaxing tasks). Significant deviations from this ideal constitute violations of justice.

The fact that in practice it will often be very difficult to fully implement this ideal does not in any way invalidate the principle itself. It simply suggests that where this occurs, some kind of compensation might be required. For example, a job with an above-average density of unpleasant or tedious work might get a higher effort rating per hour, so that a person could work fewer hours to receive the standard full time pay.

But there is another issue around balanced jobs that is not mainly about the practical difficulty of creating balanced jobs. There are situations in which people in a community may value the specific skills and contributions of certain people that they consider it a waste of the time and talents of these people for them to do as much tedious work as others. This does not imply that they should be paid more for their time or effort: the principle that pay differentials should reflect differences in effort, not contributions, is an entirely different matter. But it could well mean that the community could decide, democratically, not to strive for "balance" in the mix of tasks for some people or some kinds of jobs. This is similar to the issue of deciding to give workers extra pay for innovations, or to allow privately recruited investments for projects rejected by sector federations. Balanced jobs may best reflect the specific ideal of justice in the organization of work, but justice is not the only value people in a participatory economy will care about, and so it is reasonable for people to be willing to trade-off some deviations from justice in order to better realize some other value.

How frequent is this situation likely to be? I really have no idea. If the income consequences of such deviations are modest (because pay continues to be tied to effort), and if the amount of paid work people do decline significantly because of a broader reordering of work and leisure for both environmental and life-style reasons, then balanced jobs may simply not be an issue that people worry about so much. There is a very big difference between how salient this problem is in a world where the average work week was 15 hours compared to 40 hours.[12]

Effort Rating as the Basis for Pay Differentials

A fairly broadly held position among people holding liberal egalitarian views of justice is that inequalities due to "brute luck"—things over which one has no control—are unjust. This is fairly close to Robin's position, because it means that inequalities connected to natural talents are unjust. This also implies that inequalities in income due to education would be largely unjustified except insofar as acquiring education involves real sacrifices on the part of students, which—as Robin points out—would generally not be the case in a participatory economy in which education is free and students receive an appropriate stipend for the effort involved in their studies. Robin goes one step further by categorically rejecting any inequality connected to "contribution," even if everyone has the full opportunity to acquire the skills that enhance their productivity and thus their contribution. I broadly agree with this very general idea.[13]

---

12   It is worth noting that the massive reduction of the work week was basically Marx's conception of how this problem would be dealt with in a communist society: the "realm of necessity"—the amount of work that needed to be done to satisfy needs—would be dramatically reduced and the "realm of freedom" would expand.

13   As in the earlier discussion of Robin's potential willingness, on the grounds of incentives, to accept pay differentials for innovative behavior even though this violates effort-based pay, I assume more generally that he would regard some contribution-based pay differentials as legitimate if this was the result of a robust democratic decision.

There are a number of issues in the implementation of this ideal, however, which I do think are very difficult and which may, in the end, mean that simply paying everyone the same hourly remuneration may be better than trying to really evaluate their "effort."

Robin argues that within workplaces people generally have a pretty good idea of how much effort different workmates expend since they will all be engaged in roughly similar jobs and they closely observe each other. Workers should thus be able to make meaningful effort ratings of fellow workers. Undoubtedly this is sometimes the case, but there are many kinds of work in which it is very difficult to really know how much effort someone is expending. The problem is that the relevant meaning of "effort" for purposes of assigning remuneration is "sacrifice" or "burden." The basic idea is that in a cooperative endeavor people should equally share rewards and burdens, so if some people don't "pull their weight" then it is legitimate to reward them less. But different people can experience the exact same intensity of work as very different levels of burden. Some professors find sitting at a desk and writing intensively for eight hours exhilarating; others find it torture. This is not just that some people find writing easy and others hard; some just find it more enjoyable and exciting, and thus less of a burden. The same issue can apply to physical exertion as well: depending on one's level of fitness and one's endorphins, intense physical labor can be a greater or lesser burden. Of course, sometimes it is possible to make roughly reliable judgments that someone is goofing off, not putting their mind to the task, not trying very hard. But this probably has more to do with a sense of their lack of diligence or responsibility, than actually effort or burden or sacrifice. If the morally salient issue is paying people according to real burden, then even within workplaces this will often not at all be easy to do to.

This problem of meaningfully comparing people's efforts becomes even more intractable across workplaces, at least if different workplaces involve very different kinds of tasks.[14] I honestly don't know if

---

14 This problem of non-comparability of effort measures across workplaces is especially important because of the way aggregate effort ratings figure in all sorts of planning processes, not just individual remuneration. The resources available to a community for neighborhood public goods, for example, depend significantly on the aggregate effort rating of people in the neighborhood.

a diligent musician who practices five hours a day expends more effort or less effort than a diligent waiter in a restaurant or a diligent taxi-driver who works the same number of hours. But simply saying that the average work effort is the same across workplaces also doesn't seem plausible. I would find it an excruciating burden to collect tolls at a bridge four hours a day, but I find it a pleasure to write and lecture sixty hours a week. Which involves more "effort"? I would rather work sixty hours a week at my job than twenty hours a week as a toll collector even for the same overall pay, but many toll collectors would find it an enormous burden to spend as many hours a week as I do doing the "work" I do.[15]

I'm not sure what is the best way of dealing with these kinds of measurement problems. Robin's proposed solution to the possibility that average workplace effort levels vary significantly across workplaces is to calibrate the average effort in a workplace in terms of what he calls "the social benefit to cost ratio of each enterprise". We don't need to go into the technical details here, but basically he assumes that the only reason this ratio could be greater than 1.0 is if workers are expending more effort.[16] But as I have argued, workers may be working more intensively without this meaning that they are experiencing any greater burden or sacrifice. Paying them extra in this situation is directly paying them extra for the greater contribution they are making per hour of work (i.e. their more intense work does produce more output per hour), but not necessarily paying them more for extra burden or sacrifice. This may be desirable for motivational purposes, but it may end up being closer to a contribution-based remuneration scheme than a burden-based scheme.

Another way of assessing the burden of work in different kinds of workplace, of course, would simply be to see how difficult it is to recruit people to different work settings. To the extent that balanced jobs make work as interesting and enjoyable as possible within a

---

15 I put the word "work" in quotes here because if I were independently wealthy and my income had nothing to do with my job, I would still pretty much do exactly what I currently do connected to my job.

16 The idea is basically that if the qualities and costs of all inputs (especially labor) and outputs have been properly measured, then the only thing that could generate more total social benefit per unit of input cost would be that workers are working harder.

workplace, the main reason why it would be difficult to recruit people to some kinds of workplaces is that the work itself is over all, less attractive—i.e. more of a burden. Extra remuneration could be used then to recruit workers. This is not exactly the same sense of *effort*-burden Robin is talking about—this is more like *experience*-burden—but it still might better capture the ideal in question. It does, however, introduce something that looks more like a market mechanism for regulating the labor market: using higher wages to attract workers.

Given this array of problems, the best approximation of a remuneration system that tries to equalize the connection of rewards to burdens across workers may be simply to pay everyone the same hourly pay, perhaps with caps on the number of hours that can be counted as "work", and then allow modest deviations for pragmatic reasons.[17] This does not mean abandoning the moral premises of the burden/reward equation. This principle could still play a role of a regulative ideal in the democratic deliberations over appropriate pay schemes, but it would not be the direct basis for differentiating pay across workers and workplaces.

Concluding Comments

Robin's exploration of the normative principles and institutional designs of a participatory economy, along with his earlier joint work with Michael Albert and Albert's own treatise, *Parecon*, constitute one of the very few systematic contemporary attempts at elaborating a comprehensive model of an emancipatory alternative to capitalism. Even if it is the case that the specific institutional proposals would be unlikely to ever be adopted, even if ordinary people were fully empowered to do so, nevertheless, elements of the models should certainly be part of any sustained discussion of transcending capitalism in a

---

17 The large, successful worker-owned construction cooperative in Copenhagen, Logik & Co, pays everyone exactly the same hourly wage—from the most senior to the most junior member, regardless of skills—but does not allow anyone to be paid for more than 40 hours a week. People often work more than that, but this is treated as reflecting how much they enjoy the process. Real slackers—which are rare—are dealt with through social sanctions and, potentially, expulsion. (This information was given to me by a senior member of the cooperative during a visit there in 2012. I have not verified this account with more detailed research).

democratic, egalitarian direction. Perhaps even more crucially, since we are so distant from such a world, many of the ideas connected to participatory economics can be embodied in concrete projects of building alternative institutions inside of our existing socio-economic system.

CHAPTER 3

In Defense of Participatory Economics

Robin Hahnel

The Major Point of Contention

Let me begin by accepting Erik's characterization of our disagreement about markets. In Erik's words:

> Robin feels very confident that a complex, large-scale, well-functioning economic system . . . could exist in which markets have been completely replaced by participatory planning.

Yes, I do. Erik's writes:

> My position is that the optimal institutional configuration of a democratic-egalitarian economy is much more likely to be a mix of diverse forms of participatory planning, state regulatory mechanisms, and markets.

That is the proposal I assume Erik will defend in greater detail in round two of this dialogue. It is what I regard as a pragmatic, nuanced version of market socialism—even if Erik objects to being categorized as a market socialist—which hopefully I will criticize in the same thoughtful and comradely spirit that Erik has criticized participatory economics. Erik goes on to clarify:

> Specifically, I am skeptical that an institutional design in which markets have been completely eliminated—where they play no role whatsoever in economic coordination—is likely to be as efficient as an institutional configuration that combines a variety of forms of economic coordination: participatory planning, centralized regulations, and market interactions . . . This way of

thinking about the issues implies that the concept of 'markets' is not a binary—you either have markets or you don't.

I understand that Erik does not recommend a system where economic activity is organized by markets alone. Nonetheless, there either will be or there will not be markets in the system Erik recommends. That is a "binary" choice, to use Erik's words, about which we disagree.

At the beginning of the twentieth century, virtually all who opposed capitalism saw the market system as a destructive force that required replacement by democratic planning. Not only did they believe we needed to replace private ownership with social ownership of the "means of production," but also envisioned replacing the impersonal rule of market forces with a self-conscious system of democratic planning. During the middle third of the twentieth century, social democratic political parties changed their position on this issue, and came out in support of the view that Erik expresses above—a system that combines markets with state regulation and planning through the political system.[1] During the last fifth of the twentieth century, many radicals from the generation to which Erik and I both belong reacted to the demise of the planned economies and free market triumphalism by joining social democrats in support of a vision of "socialized markets" while endorsing the "tacit knowledge" critique of comprehensive planning voiced by conservative champions of free market capitalism like Von Mises and Hayek fifty years earlier. I believe the participatory planning procedure that is a key part of the participatory economic model demonstrates that these concessions to the practical necessity of markets were unwarranted, which is fortunate, since the pernicious effects of markets become ever more apparent as the global market system continues to spread its influence destroying community and natural environment alike.

As I said in my opening piece, the case against markets logically consists of two parts: (1) How bad are markets? (2) Is there a more

---

1   Later social democrats also dropped their opposition to private enterprise and instead favored a "mixed economy," i.e. a mixture of private and public enterprises.

desirable alternative that is feasible? Here I respond to Erik's specific criticisms of the alternative to markets we have proposed—participatory planning. I postpone until a second round in this dialogue my full argument against the use of markets until after Erik presents in more detail his case for how and why he believes markets are part of a desirable economy. But let me foreshadow my objection to markets in the broadest terms: When a division of labor is coordinated by markets, those who take advantage of others are often rewarded while those who behave in socially responsible ways are often punished for having done so. For this reason markets act like a cancer that undermines efforts to build and deepen participatory, equitable cooperation. In my view those who admire the convenience markets afford individuals fail to appreciate the magnitude of the socially destructive effects markets unleash. I claim we can provide for the desirable conveniences markets afford through participatory planning, and thereby avoid the cancerous effects market interactions have on social relations. Erik has challenged this claim in specific regards, which I will now address.

Household Consumption Planning

Erik raises two issues about household consumption planning: (1) How useful is it anyway? (2) Aren't mid-year adjustments really just forms of market behavior? In the process, he raises questions about how detailed consumption pre-ordering can or should be that other critics have raised before him. David Schweickart ridiculed household consumption planning in his book review of *Parecon: Life After Capitalism* titled "Nonsense on Stilts" in 2006. Seth Ackerman rejected participatory economics for this reason alone in "The Red and the Black" published in *Jacobin* (9) in 2013. Aware of the prevalence of this objection, Stephen Shalom made this his first question in a Q&A session with me about *Of the People, By the People* posted on the *New Politics* website on January 14, 2013. I can also testify that it has been the most frequent issue raised by students in my classes over the past twenty years when they are mulling over whether they would personally like to live in a participatory economy.

David Schweickart put it this way:

Unless requests are made in excruciating detail producers won't know what to produce. In any event, they have little motivation to find out what people really want.

Seth Ackerman thought it sufficient to dismiss comprehensive planning of any kind as a practical impossibility by simply pointing out:

> There are more than 2 million products in Amazon.com's "kitchen and dining" category alone![2]

And most recently Erik put it this way:

> The problem is that the gross categories provide virtually no useful information for the actual producers of the things I will consume. It does not help shirt-makers very much to know, based on the aggregation of individual household consumption proposals, that consumers plan to spend a certain percent of their budget on clothing; they need to have some idea of how many shirts of what style and quality to produce since these have very . . . different opportunity costs.

Since this concern features so prominently in critics' minds, let's give it a name. I'm going to call it the "size 6½, purple women's high-heeled, leatherless shoe with a yellow toe problem."

Quite simply the problem is this: A shoe producer must know to produce a size 6½, purple women's high-heeled, leatherless shoe with a yellow toe. She or he must know that size 6 will not do, a red toe will not do, a low heel will not do. However, it is unreasonable to expect the consumer who will eventually discover she or he wants a size 6½, purple women's high-heeled, leatherless shoe with a yellow toe to specify this at the beginning of the year as part of her annual consumption request.

How does a shoe producer in any economy know to produce a size 6½, purple women's high-heeled, leatherless shoe with a yellow toe, rather than a slightly different shoe? In a market economy, shoe

2   Seth Ackerman, "The Red and the Black," *Jacobin* 9 (Winter 2013).

producers guess what shoe consumers will want when they decide to go shoe shopping. They guess based on their experience. They guess based on any consumer research they engage in, perhaps including information culled from focus groups. They guess based on government projections of changes in relevant economic variables such as the distribution of income among households. And recently, many large companies have started to use newly available data-gathering and data-processing capabilities to predict what products particular customers will want in the future. When I go to the Amazon website to inquire about some book, Amazon now tells me what other books I might be interested in buying. Only when I go on the Internet from my wife's email address does Amazon provide me with book suggestions that do not match my preferences. In our brave new market economy, producers often know what we will want before we do! In market economies producers also try to influence what I will want to buy through advertising. In other words, a shoe company will decide to produce a certain style shoe and use advertising to make people want to buy the style they have decided to produce.

In sum: In market economies producers guess what to produce—because many sales are not arranged through pre-orders—and producers use advertising to try to influence consumers to buy what they have produced. New technologies of automated inventory supply line management and consumer database mining have made their guesswork more accurate, but in the end, producers are still guessing.

There is often a great deal of inefficiency that results from this guessing game that is an intrinsic feature of market economies. Unlike planned economies, in market economies there is no attempt to coordinate all the production and consumption decisions actors make, before those decisions are translated into actions. As a result a great deal of what economists call "false trading" occurs. False trades are trades individual parties make at prices that fail to equate supply and demand—which actually occurs more often than not! While seldom emphasized, competent economic theorists know that all false trading generates inefficiency to some extent, and disequilibrating forces operate in market systems alongside equilibrating forces when quantities adjust as well as prices. The notion that in market economies the convenience consumers enjoy of not having to pre-plan their consumption with producers comes at no price is based on the grossly inaccurate assumption that market economies are always in general equilibrium. For all their faults, twentieth-century planned economies did not experience major depressions, or even significant recessions caused by mutually reinforcing disequilibrating forces in markets that all too often go unchecked by sufficient countervailing fiscal and monetary policies in market economies.

But how will all this work in a participatory economy where there *is* a self-conscious attempt to coordinate production and consumption decisions before production begins?

Let's begin with information consumers will have about what is available. Ironically, the 2 million products in the Amazon.com "kitchen and dining" section is not an insurmountable problem rendering comprehensive economic planning of any kind impossible at all. Instead it is a wonderful example of how consumers today can easily be made aware of the tremendous variety of products that will be available in a participatory economy. Just as Amazon.com can list millions of products—providing pictures and details about their characteristics—consumer federations can provide this service to consumers in a participatory economy for any who wish to shop online. And for those who prefer what some of my students once told me were "the pleasures of malling it," consumer federations can host shopping malls where anyone who wishes can go to see and be seen, and walk away with whatever strikes their fancy. Information about product improvements can be provided by consumer federations as well. The fact that it will be consumer federations providing information about products, rather than producers singing their own praises as is the case in market economies, seems to me to be a significant change for the better.[3] But, how, critics ask, will consumers pre-order?

It is important to distinguish between what we need to accomplish and what we do not need to accomplish in the annual participatory planning process. When the year starts, any shoemaking worker council with an approved proposal knows it should start making

---

3   We have also suggested that consumer federations be primarily responsible for research and development of new and better products in a participatory economy, rather than leave product innovation to producers as is it is in market economies.

shoes. It also knows how much cloth, leather, rubber, etc. it has been pre-authorized for during the year, and how many shoes it has said it can make. It also knows that X percent of the shoes it made last year were women's shoes, and Y percent of the women's shoes it made last year were size 6½. How does it know whether to make size 6½, purple women's high-heeled, leatherless shoes with a yellow toe, or size 6½, purple women's high-heeled, leatherless shoe with a red toe? It does just what a shoemaking company in a market economy does: It makes an educated guess. Then, as soon as actual consumption begins new information becomes available. Suppose purchases of size 6½, purple women's high-heeled, leatherless shoes with a yellow toe are lower than producers expected while the red-toed shoes are disappearing like hot cakes. This kind of new information is what helps worker councils answer the question of exactly what kind of shoe I should be producing, just as it does in market economies. So much for the claim that a planned economy has no answer to the size 6½, purple women's high-heeled, leatherless shoe with a yellow toe problem. It has the same answer a market system does with regard to moving from a "coarse" decision about shoe production to a "detailed" decision about the production of a size 6½, purple women's high-heeled, leatherless shoe with a yellow toe.

This first kind of new information fills in the details producers need to know about exactly what kinds of shoes people want, which is why consumers do not need to specify these details when submitting their personal consumption requests during the planning procedure. Submitting personal consumption requests during planning is not impossibly burdensome because the form would only need to have an entry called "shoes" for one to put a number after, not an entry called "size 6½, purple women's high-heeled, leatherless shoes with a yellow toe!" Those kinds of details are revealed by actual purchases as the year proceeds. In other words, Erik misreads our proposal when he writes: "Since the coarse categories would not be useful for planning by federations of worker councils, and this is the fundamental purpose for pre-ordering consumption, I will assume that the finest level of detail is required." Consumption proposals during planning are made using what Erik calls "coarse categories" because the fine level of detail that producers require is revealed as the plan is actually implemented. Whether filling out even this reduced list of items is beyond people's capabilities or desires I will return to shortly.[4]

What about David Schweickart's claim that worker councils "have little motivation to find out what people really want," disenfranchising consumers as the centrally planned Soviet economy certainly did for decades? Here it is important to distinguish between the worker-council production plan that was approved as "socially responsible" before the year began, and what the worker council is credited for at the end of the year. Plan approval is based on projected social benefit to cost ratios. However, worker councils are credited for the social benefit to cost ratio of actual outputs delivered and accepted, and actual inputs used during the year.[5]

It is last year's *actual* social benefit to cost ratio that serves as a cap on average effort ratings worker councils can award members. So if their approved production plan had a SB/SC ratio of 1.09 but their actual ratio at year's end turns out to be 1.03, the cap on average effort ratings for workers in the council next year is 1.03, not 1.09. Therefore, a worker council that failed to reduce yellow-toed-shoe production and increase red-toed-shoe production in response to signals that become available during the year about what consumers truly like would end up with a lower actual social benefit to cost ratio, and consequently a lower average effort rating for the following year.[6]

---

4   If a consumer knows she wants women's shoes, or size 6½ shoes, there is no reason for her not to add this information when filling out her consumption order—since it is useful for producers. The point is simply that she does not have to if this is too burdensome, and she can change her mind later if she wants.

5   Similarly, consumers, and consumer councils and federations are charged for what they actually consume during the year, not what was approved for them in the plan. Any differences are recorded as increases or decreases in the debt or savings of individual consumers, neighborhood councils, and consumer federations.

6   There are endless details one could pursue in this, as in other areas, regarding exactly how a participatory economy would actually function. Suppose a worker council delivers yellow-toed shoes to the consumer federation. Suppose the consumer federation accepts them anticipating that they will sell, only to discover later that nobody bought them because they bought red-toed shoes instead. Who takes responsibility? Does the worker council get credit for them because they were accepted by the consumer federation? Or does the consumer federation notify the worker council at the end of the year that it does not get credit for some of the yellow-toed shoes it produced? Selling is different from selling on consignment. The important question is not which option will be

Actual purchase patterns during the year reveal more than needed details about consumer desires. They also signal when consumers have changed their minds. At the individual level people reveal by their purchases that they want more of some things and less of others than they indicated during planning. At the aggregate level individual increases and decreases sometimes cancel out and therefore require no changes in production. When they do not cancel out, how to increase or decrease production of shoes because consumers have changed their minds must be negotiated between the shoe industry federation and the national consumer federation. Again, there are different ways these adjustments could be handled, each with its pros and cons. But the relevant point is that adjustments can be made.[7] The difference between a planned economy and an unplanned market economy is that, to the extent that consumers submit proposals that reflect their changed circumstances and tastes, and to the extent that worker councils submit proposals that reflect their new technologies and work preferences, the plan creates an initial situation that reduces the number and size of adjustments that are necessary. All mechanisms for making adjustments in a market economy are available, if wanted, in a planned economy as well, although presumably a participatory economy would put a higher priority on using mechanisms that distribute the costs of adjustments more fairly.

Finally, how burdensome is it for consumers to put numbers next to a list of "coarse categories?" Perhaps I was too flip when I explained

---

chosen—because that will be decided by the people who live in a participatory economy. The issue before us now is simply if there are perfectly straightforward solutions to these problems, and therefore a participatory economy is, indeed, a practical possibility.

7　The crucial questions are: (1) To what extent will the shoe industry or consumers bear the burden of adjustments? (2) Will shoe customers who change their demand for shoes be treated any differently from shoe customers who do not? In the case of excess supply, the issue reduces to whether or not producers will be credited for shoes that are added to inventories, and if so how much. The case of excess demand is more complicated. To raise shoe production, more resources will have to be drawn out of inventories or away from industries experiencing excess supply. Beyond crediting shoe workers for working longer hours, will the indicative prices of shoes and those resources be increased above their levels in the plan, or not? If shoe production is not raised sufficiently to satisfy all who now want shoes, will those who did not increase their demand above what they ordered be given preference?

in my most recent book how a lazy person such as myself might spend no time on submitting a new consumption request without impinging on the ability of my neighborhood council to participate in the planning procedure, and without serious personal repercussions. If a person does not fill out and submit a consumption request form, their neighborhood council can simply use their actual consumption last year as their new consumption request for this year. If their effort rating for this year warrants this level of consumption, their request will be approved and included in the neighborhood proposal. If not, and if a person continues to fail to respond to requests for a new proposal, the neighborhood council can reduce every item in their last year consumption by the same percent until the reduced request is covered by their lower effort rating this year. In this way, neighborhood consumption councils, who must submit neighborhood proposals during the planning procedure, can do what they have to do even if some of their members fail to provide personal consumption proposals.

In the end Erik seems to understand how signaling necessary details to producers and making adjustments because consumers changed their minds can work in a participatory economy. He writes:

> Production . . . in effect would be done pretty much as . . . now: producers would examine the sales and trends of sales in the recent past, and make their best estimate of what to produce . . . on that basis. Indeed, since producers and their sector federations can continually and efficiently monitor these trends, they are in a position to make updates to plans in an ongoing way on the basis of the actual behavior of consumers, rather than mainly organize their planning activities around annual plans animated by uninformative household pre-orders.

This is accurate enough, although I don't see why Erik dismisses household pre-orders as "uninformative." They certainly provide industry federations more useful information at the start of the year than the zero information market systems provide producers about changes in consumer intentions.

From year to year consumers' incomes change, and consumers' desires change. Signaling producers about these changes is what pre-ordering is for and why it is quite useful for producers. Necessary details can be filled in from consumer profiles and actual purchases during the year, and adjustments can be negotiated with the aid of instantaneous inventory supply line prompts at the disposal of worker councils and federations. But just because pre-ordering lacks detail and people change their minds does not mean the planning process is pointless. If we want consumers to influence what is produced in the economy, and if we are going to decide what is produced in large part through a planning procedure, then we need consumers to provide their best guesses about what they will want. We don't need them to agonize over their proposals, and we certainly can accommodate them when they change their minds.

Erik also asks:

> I don't understand why my personal consumption should be the business of a neighborhood council, even apart from the problem already discussed of the usefulness of the procedures involved.

This question has been raised before, and fortunately, therefore, I have a name for it. I call it the "kinky underwear problem." One may not want one's neighbors gossiping about what kind of underwear one has ordered.[8] In recent expositions, I have tried to explain that it was never our intent that one's neighbors should sit in judgment over one's consumption requests, and offered several suggestions for how consumer privacy could be protected. The bottom line is that personal consumption requests must be approved or disapproved, and this must occur before neighborhood consumption councils can submit their aggregated neighborhood consumption requests during the planning procedure. Since neighborhood councils must aggregate their members' approved requests we talked about them as also approving them. But even in our earliest presentation we specified that as long as one's effort rating plus any allowance was sufficient to cover the social cost of one's request, it could not be denied. In 1991

8　Since one simply puts a number after the category "underwear" when submitting personal consumption requests, kinky underwear is really not an issue—although the point remains: Why should one's neighbors pass judgment on one's consumption request?

we also wrote of neighbors having the opportunity to provide constructive feedback and suggestions about particulars, which in retrospect was probably overly enthusiastic on our part. Over the years it has become apparent, at least to me, that for most people today concern for privacy is far greater than any desire for constructive feedback from one's neighbors.

In any case, there are a number of ways to protect privacy. (1) Eliminate review and make approval or disapproval of individual consumption requests automatic based on effort rating and allowances—which seems to be Erik's preference. (2) There is no reason to attach names to personal consumption proposals. Review only requires an effort rating, an allowance, and a personal consumption request form that is filled out. Submissions can be by number, not name. (3) Personal requests—with or without names attached—could be reviewed by consumption councils that are not geographically based. So any information about one's consumption request would be available only to strangers. In this case the decision to approve or disapprove would have to be passed on from the non-geographical council to one's neighborhood consumption council so it could be added to other individual requests and requests for neighborhood public goods.

Similar issues arise regarding who approves special needs requests and requests for loans. To enhance building strong, local, neighborhood communities, we suggested that special needs requests and loan applications be handled by one's neighborhood consumption council. But that is not the only option. These functions could be delocalized if people felt that was more advantageous.

Finally, is the adjustment process really just a market after all, as Erik suggests? Approved consumption plans are not treated as binding contracts since individuals are free to change their minds as the year proceeds. One possible option for making adjustments would allow indicative prices to rise when excess demand for something appears during the year, and indicative prices to fall in the case of excess supply. If it looks like a market, and smells like a market, doesn't that mean it is a market?

In this case the answer is "no." Here are the crucial differences:

(1) In market economies, there is no plan that has been agreed to at the beginning of the year. There is no plan where people had an

opportunity to affect production and consumption decisions, at least roughly in proportion to the degree they are affected. There is no plan that incorporates effects on "external parties," which are ignored by buyers and sellers who make the decisions in market economies. There is no plan that would be efficient, fair, and environmentally sustainable if carried out. Instead, in a market economy all decisions about how to organize a division of labor and distribute the benefits from having done so are settled by agreements between buyer-seller pairs—which predictably leads to outcomes that are inequitable, inefficient, and environmentally unsustainable.

(2) Even when adjustments are made during the year in a participatory economy, individual buyers and sellers do not negotiate those adjustments between themselves however they see fit, including any adjustment in prices. Instead, adjustments are negotiated socially. Industry and consumer federations negotiate adjustments in production. And whether or not to adjust indicative prices is also a social decision, so that fairness as well as efficiency can be taken into account.

Markets are the aggregate sum of haggling between many self-selected pairs of buyer-seller. Neither participatory planning nor the adjustment procedures I have discussed above permit self-selected buyer-seller pairs to make whatever deals they want—because we have learned that the consequences of allowing this are unacceptable.

Public Goods Planning

As Erik says, we are in substantial agreement about how to plan for public goods consumption. He is correct that once it is decided how much of consumers' income will go toward private versus public consumption, approval of private consumption requests could be handled outside neighborhood consumption councils. I have already explained why designating neighborhood councils to handle private consumption requests, as well as requests based on special needs and requests for loans, seems to be a good way to build strong local communities, but all these decisions could be de-localized if people wanted to.

Erik is also correct when he observes that many functions performed by what we call political institutions today are undertaken by consumer federations in a participatory economy. That is because markets cannot be relied on to provide adequate amounts of public goods, so different levels of "government" must step in and do this through public expenditures on public goods paid for by taxes. In effect, market economies fail utterly to provide public goods, so in the most egregious cases people have come to insist that government institutions fill this void, even if very imperfectly. Since we consider public goods to be just as much a part of "the economy" as private goods, we have proposed economic institutions and procedures to handle them, which we believe also eliminates the unfortunate bias in market economies against public goods and in favor of private goods consumption.

I don't see the distinction Erik tries to draw between consumer public goods and citizen public goods. Not all goods that are public are public for the same reason and the same way. And "yes," each of us is consumer, producer, and citizen. And "yes," there will still be a need for an appropriate set of political institutions to handle political issues besides the institutions we have proposed to handle economic decisions.[9] But I don't see any purpose in setting up a separate network of citizen councils to demand citizen public goods. Even if this were done, presumably these councils would function just as our consumer federations do, and they would have to participate in the participatory planning process, making and revising proposals in every round.

Externalities
In free-market economies, externalities go completely unaccounted for—effectively disenfranchising external parties who have no say in deals struck by buyers and sellers. This not only generates a great deal of inefficiency, it is increasingly obvious that it is putting the natural environment seriously at risk. While it is possible to ameliorate damage due to external effects through regulation, emission taxes, or cap and trade policies, the problem remains that the market system provides no signals as to how much correction is warranted. It is well

---

9 Stephen Shalom has proposed a set of political institutions that he argues are compatible with the values and goals of a participatory economy, which is sometimes referred to as "parpolity."

known that in theory if we set an emission tax equal to the sum of the negative effects on all external parties we will get the efficient level of emissions. However, the market provides no information about the magnitude of damages caused and therefore how high such a tax should be. Moreover, *ad hoc* corrections in every market that are inherently contestable soon become highly impractical. As Erik acknowledges, one of the more interesting features of participatory planning is how it handles externalities. As I explained in my initial presentation, by having communities of affected parties participate in the planning procedure as described we are able to generate reasonably accurate quantitative estimates of damages from emissions, which worker councils can then be charged for, just as they are charged for using scarce productive resources.

Erik points out: "The geographical boundaries of a particular source of pollution may or may not correspond to the boundaries of existing consumer federations."

Erik is absolutely correct. Additional "communities of affected parties," or CAPs, would have to be created whenever the effects of pollution do not conform to areas already defined as neighborhood consumer councils or federations, which adds a whole new institutional layer to the economy. Moreover, I have acknowledged that the most difficult problem with our proposal for how to handle externalities will be settling on membership in CAPs.[10] For the record, I have stated:

Since membership in a CAP entitles one to extra consumption rights, a serious problem will be that people may claim to be adversely affected and deserve membership in a CAP even though they are not. This means the process of defining CAPs—deciding who should, and who should not be included—must be carefully monitored. It might even be necessary to create a formal "judicial" system for settling disputes over membership in CAPs. Presumably, expert testimony of scientists and medical personnel would be relevant, along with testimony on the part of

---

10 This and other issues Erik raises are treated at length in "Wanted: A Pollution Damage Revealing Mechanism," available from me upon request and under review at the *Review of Radical Political Economics*.

individuals petitioning for membership, as well as testimony from current members contesting their claims.

Unfortunately, there appears to be no way around this. Erik asks:

> Would coalitions of most affected consumers be able to constitute themselves as an ad hoc federation and insist on higher prices for the rights to pollute? . . . Could they constitute a blocking coalition?

No. This is a misunderstanding of how the procedure works. Once membership in a CAP has been settled—through what may sometimes be a contested judicial process as explained above—the CAP must come up with a single answer to how many units of the pollutant they are willing to permit given the level of compensation quoted. Disagreements among members of CAPs about how much to allow must be hashed out among themselves—presumably through discussion where people try to persuade others to agree with them, but ultimately determined by democratic vote. There will be disagreements among members of CAPs over how the CAP should respond, just as there will be disagreements among members of consumer councils and federations over how much of any public good to request. But just as members of consumer councils and federations who have different preferences and opinions must come up with a single answer for which public goods to request, and how much, so must members of a CAP with different attitudes about pollution come up with a single answer to how much pollution they are willing to permit.

A different issue is whether the compensation paid the CAP will be distributed equally among all its members. I have addressed this issue at greater length in an article soon to appear.[11] The simple solution is to distribute equal shares to all members of a CAP, in which case everyone has an incentive to report truthfully how much they believe they will be damaged. However, if members of a CAP wished to pay greater compensation to members who are more adversely affected they could do so without distorting incentives to report damage by

---

11   Ibid.

using any of several "incentive compatible mechanisms" that are now part of the public good literature. The key to incentive compatibility is that the formula for determining an individual's compensation must *not* use the individual's own reported damage. As ingenious as they are, I suspect people would usually find these incentive compatible procedures for distributing compensation unequally among members of CAPs to be more trouble than they are worth. Erik says:

> Unless I am misunderstanding the process involved, the procedures Robin advocates would likely generate considerable heterogeneity in the pollution taxes (i.e. the negative externality charges built into "indicative prices") faced by producers of similar goods in different places. This means producers in areas where consumers don't care so much about pollution would be able to produce at lower cost. However, there is no restriction (as far as I can tell) that they only distribute their products to the pollution-indifferent consumers. This means that the same goods will be available to consumers elsewhere at lower and higher indicative prices depending on the pollution preferences of consumers in the places where production takes place. This begins to look like a situation that generates market pressures on the high cost producers.

While true that in Portland, Oregon firms may be charged a higher amount for a ton of particulate matter released than firms in Dallas, Texas, this does not produce the problem Erik worries about. What it does is induce firms releasing particulate matter to locate in Dallas rather than in Portland. The charge is higher in Portland either because Portland is hemmed in between the Coastal and Cascade Mountains so the particulate matter stays in the air longer than in Dallas where the prairie wind sweeps it away faster, or because Portlanders value clean air more than the residents of Dallas. In either case, our best estimate of the social cost of particulate emissions in Portland is higher than in Dallas, and that is a signal we want to send particulate emitters when they are deciding where to locate.

What happens when a worker council building houses in Portland needs cement? There will be a single indicative price for cement nationwide, which it will be charged for each ton it uses no matter the source. But where will the cement come from? A Portland cement factory, or a cement factory in Dallas? If the social cost of transporting the cement from Dallas to Portland is less than the higher social cost of producing cement in Portland because the charge for releasing particulate matter in Portland is higher, the cement will come from Dallas. Otherwise it will come from Portland.

Finally, Erik suggests:

Consumers might decide that they prefer a simpler system which combines government regulations that impose various kinds of limits on allowable pollution with a system of uniform taxes on different types of environmental externalities.

Simpler is always better, all other things being equal. But in this case other things are not equal. Government regulations mean limiting emissions. But how much should the government require polluters to reduce emissions? Say, 5 percent, 10 percent, 30 percent, 70 percent? A market system provides no help when we try to answer the "how much" question. A uniform tax on each type of pollution? The example above demonstrates why the same tax on particulate emissions in Portland and Dallas is actually wrong. But even if a uniform tax on particulate emissions nationwide were efficient, how high should the tax be? Should it be $5 a ton, $10 a ton, $30 a ton, $70 a ton? Again, the market system provides no help when we try to answer the "how high" question. The beauty of the procedure we have proposed, as Erik acknowledged, is that it generates a credible quantitative estimate of how high emissions charges should be, and induces players to emit socially efficient quantities as a result. It is true that you don't get this major advantage at no cost. But the cost reduces to spending some extra time and resources to set up a judicial procedure to settle foreseeable disputes over membership in communities of affected parties.

There is actually one other "cost"—although I think Erik will agree with me that it is actually not a "cost" but a "benefit." Our mechanism doesn't work if communities have significantly different incomes because it would lead to a race to the bottom effect where pollution was unfairly and inefficiently located nearer poor communities. Only in a highly egalitarian economy such as the participatory economy we propose does it appear possible to design a mechanism that reveals accurate quantitative estimates of the damage from pollution.

Risk and Innovation

Any group of workers who can submit a proposal during the planning procedure that is approved as socially responsible, i.e. whose social benefit to cost ratio is at least one, will receive the inputs it requests to start producing when the year begins. That could be a group composed mostly of students exiting the educational system. It could be a group of disgruntled members of an existing worker council who have been consistently outvoted about how to do things, and who want to start up a new operation to try and do things their own way. The problem is how to protect others from negative consequences if a group of crackpots submit a proposal that looks good and is approved, but in fact is a fantasy because they will not be able to comply with their promise? If this happens, at a minimum, resources will be wasted and, in all likelihood, other worker councils who rely on deliveries from the crackpots that do not arrive will be unable to fulfill their plans through no fault of their own. That is what I meant when I wrote that it seems wise to empower industry federations to verify the credibility of new groups asking to participate in the planning process. By "credible" I simply meant "not obvious crackpots."

I sympathize with Erik's concern that industry federations might be too conservative in these judgments, and act like old fuddy-duddies who stifle creative new ideas. And I would look kindly on any suggestions to prevent this from happening. What I do not agree with is Erik's tendency to interpret democracy with regard to economic system design as "anything any group in the economy wants to do should be permitted rather than disallowed." There will be people in a participatory economy who want to start up a privately-owned firm, hire employees, and keep the profits. When a solid majority disapprove of this kind of economic relationship, I think they have every right to outlaw it. It has no place in a participatory, equitable economy. It is inconsistent with economic self-management for the employees, and when wages commensurate with sacrifices are not forthcoming, it will be inconsistent with economic justice as well. Crowdsourcing where investors earn a return on their investments, which Erik regards positively, might melt the glue of economic justice that holds a participatory economy together. It could create the same problem the Cuban government creates every time it succumbs to pressure to appease frustrated Cuban entrepreneurial desires by allowing people to start up small businesses for profit. When a trained doctor stops doctoring in Cuba to drive a private taxi, and earns ten times more a week from doing so than his fellow doctors who continue to work in public clinics, it makes those colleagues feel like suckers. What Cuba has long needed to do instead is to allow frustrated Cuban workers to self-manage their own workplaces, and allow Cubans with frustrated entrepreneurial ideas opportunities to start up new worker self-managed enterprises that balance jobs and reward effort.

But there is also a practical problem with Erik's suggestions about risk and innovation when applied in the context of a participatory economy. Even if those who received start-up funds from crowd-sourcing agreed that the enterprise would be run according to participatory economic principles, and even if investors received no return on their investment, the new enterprise would have to obtain the inputs it needs to operate through the participatory planning procedure. And it can't do this without being certified as "credible." A worker council can't buy its inputs with funds raised through crowd-sourcing in a participatory economy.

I think, instead, what is needed are multiple ways for groups who want to start up new enterprises to demonstrate their credibility so they can participate in the planning procedure. If a group comes with an impressive display of crowdsourcing support, this can demonstrate credibility. If members of the group have relevant educational credentials, this can demonstrate credibility. If members of the group have worked in the industry elsewhere, this can demonstrate credibility. Another option would be to create a review board, separate from all the industry federations, where groups who were turned down for accreditation by their industry federation could appeal for approval. We could even order this board to overturn rulings until the number of new firms they approved who turned out to be crackpots reached some specified percentage—demonstrating that we were no longer being too conservative in accrediting start-ups.

It seems to me better to think along these lines than to think about adding a dose of capitalist investment to a participatory economy. Not only is this a practical impossibility because of the way all enterprises must obtain their inputs, but also unnecessary and destructive of equitable cooperation.

The Organization of Work and Pay

Erik and I are clearly in broad agreement on these issues. He writes: "I fully support the central ideas of Robin's framework for both the organization of work and for pay: balanced jobs and pay determined by effort rather than contribution." As I noted earlier, many prominent market socialists do not support either balancing jobs or pay according to effort rather than contribution, so it is gratifying to have an ally on these issues, which are highly contested at this point even among those who see themselves as staunch "leftists."

Moreover, since I was never under any illusions that balancing jobs and rewarding effort would always be easy to achieve, I welcome discussion about difficulties that will arise in what Erik calls "the practical implementation of the ideals."

As I see it there are two practical problems: (1) There will be people in a participatory economy who disagree with the principles. What does one do when workers in an enterprise want to reward contribution rather than effort? What does one do when workers in an enterprise don't want to balance jobs? (2) Even if everyone did agree on balancing jobs and rewarding effort, sometimes it will be difficult to accomplish because effort, empowerment, and/or desirability can be difficult to measure.

Regarding the first problem: Supporters of participatory economics *recommend* that worker councils *try* to balance jobs and reward effort *as best they can, taking practical obstacles into account*. However, we *propose* to leave this up to individual worker councils to work out as they see fit, and we would oppose any proposals authorizing anyone outside a workplace to impose these policies on a workplace where a majority of members did not wish to implement them. This is why we expect that different worker councils will go about things quite differently. For example, some may decide to do just what Erik suggests might prove reasonable in some cases—pay everyone the same rate of pay per hour they work.

What does one do then when a majority of members of a worker council want to reward contribution rather than effort? What does one do when a majority don't want to balance jobs? And, "yes," it seems likely that in the early years of a participatory economy there will be worker councils where those favoring balancing jobs and rewarding effort will be in the minority. To effect a full transition to an economy that is truly based on economic justice and democracy, at least two things will be necessary: First and foremost, other workers in the same enterprise must argue with these workmates, explaining to them why failing to balance jobs will erode effectively equal rights to participate in workplace decisions, and why rewarding contribution rather than effort will be unfair to some members. Secondly, political groups who champion economic democracy and justice must wage fierce ideological campaigns on these subjects. There must be an ongoing national dialogue on these issues driven by political parties and interest groups, facilitated by the formal political and educational systems, until what may start as a slim majority who support these principles nationwide has become an overwhelming majority. It will be of great importance that such a national debate form the backdrop for discussions that will rage inside individual worker councils.[12] But we believe, and I suspect Erik agrees, any attempt to impose these principles on unwilling workers will only prove counterproductive.[13]

Regarding measuring effort: I admit it is sometimes difficult to measure effort, or sacrifice, and confine myself only to clarifying one issue that is understandably confusing. For interested readers, this

---

12 Popular opinion in Cuba about what constituted fair pay was changed dramatically in less than ten years after the revolution by just the kind of ideological and educational campaigns I am talking about. By the late 1960s most Cubans believed that those who had the good fortune to receive more education owed society more, rather than being owed more by society. Unfortunately, attitudes about economic justice may have retrogressed somewhat in Cuba since then.

13 As indicated previously, I do not believe this principle should be applied to minorities who want to set up private businesses for profit. A participatory economy is an economy where the role of employer is outlawed, just as the role of slave owner has been outlawed everywhere in the United States since June 19, 1965. But as long as every worker in a worker council has one vote, I believe each worker council should be permitted to decide how to organize work and how to reward one another as they see fit.

problem is addressed at greater length in *Of the People, By the People*.

Erik writes:

> Different people can experience the exact same intensity of work as very different levels of burden. Some professors find sitting at a desk and writing intensively for eight hours exhilarating; others find it torture.

And:

> I would find it an excruciating burden to collect tolls at a bridge four hours a day, but I find it a pleasure to write and lecture sixty hours a week. Which involves more "effort"? I would rather work sixty hours a week at my job than twenty hours a week as a toll collector even for the same overall pay, but many toll collectors would find it an enormous burden to spend as many hours a week as I do doing the "work" I do.[14]

Consider this: Just as some people like apples more than oranges while other people like oranges more than apples, some people like mowing lawns more than washing windows (me) while other people like washing windows more than mowing lawns (my eldest son). It would have been crazy—economists call it "inefficient"—for me to have washed the windows and my son to have mowed the lawn at our house. It would have been less crazy, but nonetheless still crazy for each of us to mow and wash half the time. So of course we agreed that I would mow four hours a week and he would wash four hours a week—*and our jobs were balanced for both desirability and empowerment!*

What's the trick? Mowing lawns and washing windows are more or less equally unempowering. Mowing lawns and washing windows are more or less equally undesirable *for the average person.* Clearly they are not equally undesirable for either me or my son; and an hour spent mowing would have been a bigger sacrifice for my son than for

---

14   David Kotz raised similar concerns in his contribution to a symposium on the future of socialism published in *Science and Society* 66, no. 1 (Spring 2002).

me, just as an hour of washing windows would have been a bigger sacrifice for me than for him. But if you advertise window-washing and lawn-mowing jobs for the same rate of pay, the line of applicants for each job would be roughly the same length, and that is the sense in which we call them equally undesirable forms of human activity (as compared to leisure).

Erik should clearly not apply for a job collecting tolls in a participatory economy, any more than I should have washed windows at my house. However, *because on average people would rather write and lecture than collect tolls,* Erik should be compensated somewhat less for an hour of professor work than a toll worker is compensated for an hour of toll collection   whether or not practical complications make this easy to measure and achieve in a participatory economy. Nor should we be overly pessimistic about our ability to measure differences in desirability. When applicants are few, a job is probably less desirable than average, and some less desirable tasks need to be replaced by more desirable ones; and when applicants are many, a job is probably more desirable than average, and some desirable tasks need to be replaced by less desirable ones.

Conclusion

The initial purpose of elaborating the model of a participatory economy was to demonstrate concretely that at least in theory, the presumption that had become increasingly widespread even among leftists, that we must choose between authoritarian planning or a market economy, is wrong. There is a third alternative—which turns out to look very much like the kind of economy socialists envisioned long ago, but were only able to describe in a general way that many no longer found convincing. But the model of a participatory economy—which I believe demonstrates that the original socialist vision was not a pipe dream, but perfectly possible—should not be confused with a transition strategy, much less a political program. A participatory economy is only a coherent answer to how a full-fledged system of equitable cooperation might function—without recourse to authoritarian planning or markets. How to go about replacing the increasingly destructive economics of competition and greed with an economics of equitable cooperation is a different, more difficult question.

PART TWO

CHAPTER 4

Socialism and Real Utopias

Erik Olin Wright[1]

In what follows I will outline a general way of thinking about alternatives to capitalism that is anchored in two ideas: *real utopias* and *socialism*. Real utopia identifies institutional designs that simultaneously attempt to embody emancipatory ideals in a serious way while still being attentive to the practical problems of viability and sustainability. Socialism, of course, is a venerable term associated with anti-capitalist struggles, but to many critics of capitalism it has lost its appeal, both because of its association with the authoritarian state-run economic systems of the twentieth century and its association with many political parties in developed capitalist countries that have abandoned any ambition of transcending capitalism. In spite of this, because of its clear historical association with anti-capitalism, I will propose a reconstruction of the idea of socialism that, when combined with the idea of real utopias, can offer a framework for both a vision beyond capitalism and the practical work of moving in that direction.

To set the stage for this discussion, it will be helpful to begin by briefly examining the very idea of an "alternative" to the existing social world. This will be followed by a discussion of a particular way of thinking about socialism in which the "social" in socialism is taken seriously. We will then turn to the idea of "real utopias" as a way of framing the problem of transforming—and transcending—capitalism.

Thinking about Systemic Alternatives

One of the striking things about human imagination is our capacity to think that things could be otherwise, whether the objects of such

---

1   Parts of this essay are taken from "Transforming Capitalism through Real Utopias," *American Sociological Review* 78, *no. 1* (February 2012): 1–25.

imagination are our immediate life circumstances or the broader society in which we live.[2] Such imagination, fuelled by deep longing, easily drifts into wishful thinking, fantasies of what a better world would be like unconstrained by difficult questions of whether such imagined alternatives would actually work. Wishful thinking can help provide motivation for action, but it can also lead to dead ends and disillusion. What we need, then, is utopian longing melded to realist thinking about the dilemmas and constraints of building viable alternatives to the world as it is.

My strategy for exploring these questions is rooted in three very general considerations about the nature of social systems and the problem of transforming them.

First, what precisely does the word "system" mean when we talk about "social systems"? This is a big theme in social theory, one filled with opaque formulations. For present purposes, a contrast between two metaphors for thinking about systems can be helpful. One metaphor conceives of a society as analogous to an organism in which all of its parts are tightly integrated into a functioning whole. There is some degree of freedom and variability in the way the parts function, but basically the component parts of an organism constitute a totality of functional interdependency. If you remove critical parts of the whole or try to dramatically transform them, the whole disintegrates.

An alternative metaphor is that a social system is more like an ecosystem. Think of society like a pond. A pond contains many species of fish, insects, and plants within a specific watershed, terrain, and climate. Sometimes an alien species gets introduced into the ecosystem and it thrives; sometimes it does not. Some ecosystems are quite fragile and easily disrupted; others can tolerate quite significant intrusions of invasive species without being seriously affected. If you think of society as an ecosystem, it still is the case that everything is interdependent, everything affects everything in one way or another, but the system does not constitute a tightly functionalized totality.

---

2   For a superb discussion of the utopian imagination, see Ruth Levitas, *Utopia as Method: The Imaginary Reconstitution of Society* (Hampshire: Palgrave MacMillan, 2013), particularly her discussion of Ernst Bloch. Bloch, Levitas writes, "posited the existence of a utopian impulse, an anthropological given that underpins the human propensity to long for and imagine a life otherwise."

This opens up a different way of imagining alternatives. One way to transform an ecosystem is to introduce an alien species that initially finds a niche and then gradually increases, potentially even displacing certain other species. The idea of real utopias as a way of transforming a society is more in line with the ecosystem view of society than the organismic view.

The second general comment about alternatives concerns two contrasting ways of thinking about how to make the world a better place—*ameliorative reforms* and *real utopian transformations*. Ameliorative reforms involve looking at existing institutions, identifying their flaws and proposing improvements that can be enacted. These improvements matter—they reduce harms and enhance flourishing—but they are limited to those improvements that directly act on existing structures and move one step beyond. Real utopias, in contrast, envision the contours of an alternative social world that embodies emancipatory ideals and then look for social innovations we can create in the world as it is that move us towards that destination. Now sometimes this turns out to be the same as an ameliorative reform, but often ameliorative reforms do not constitute building blocks of an emancipatory alternative. Consider, for example, affirmative action policies around race. Affirmative action is one of the critical policies for combating the pernicious effects of ongoing racism, not merely the legacies of racism in the past. But affirmative action is not itself a building block of a world of racial justice and emancipation. It is a necessary means to neutralize severe harms of racism in the world as it exists, but it is not itself a constitutive element of the alternative that we seek. The same could be said of food stamps: it is a critical policy for alleviating hunger generated by brutal forms of inequality generated in American capitalism, but the imagined world of social emancipation beyond capitalism is not one characterized by a massive expansion of food stamps for all. Real utopian transformations, in contrast, consist of building elements of the alternative world we seek in the world as it is.

Finally, there is the difficult problem of deciding how much concrete detail to try to specify in exploring the alternative social system of our utopian longing. One impulse is try to create a detailed account of the critical institutions of an alternative system and making arguments about how these would actually work. This can be in the spirit of trying to paint a vivid, compelling picture of what it would be like to live in such an alternative world rather than providing a rigid recipe of how to build a new society, but often such efforts look something like a contrived blueprint for emancipatory institutions and practices. An alternative impulse is to enunciate the basic values that animate the search for alternatives and the core principles of institutional design that would facilitate a realization of those values, but not attempt a comprehensive, integrated design model of the alternative system as a whole.

Both of these strategies have value. The detailed model-building strategy is useful and sometimes inspiring, so long as one treats these as speculative ideas to inform the messy trial-and-error experimentation of emancipatory social transformation rather than blueprints. The more open-ended discussion of general principles and values can help give us a sense of the direction we want to move and provide a basis for critical evaluation of our experiments, but provides less clarity of what it might be like to live in the destination itself. This is the strategy I will pursue here.

A Social Socialism

Both social democracy and socialism contain the word "social," but generally this term is invoked in a loose and ill-defined way. The suggestion is of a political program committed to the broad welfare of society rather than the narrow interests of particular elites. Sometimes, especially in more radical versions of socialist discourse, "social ownership" of the means of production is invoked as a contrast to "private ownership," but in practice this has generally been collapsed into state ownership, and the term social itself ends up doing relatively little analytical work in the elaboration of the political program. What I will argue is that the social in social democracy and socialism can be used to identify a cluster of principles and visions of change that differentiate socialism and social democracy from both the capitalist project of economic organization and what could be called a purely statist response to capitalism.

At the center of the analysis is a power-centered framework for understanding capitalism and its alternatives. Power is an especially elusive and contested concept in social theory, often formulated in ways that make it very difficult to use in concrete discussions of institutions and their transformation. In the present context, I will adopt a deliberately stripped-down concept of power: power is the capacity to do things in the world, to produce effects. This is what might be called an "agent-centered" notion of power: people, both acting individually and collectively, use power to accomplish things.

With this broad definition of power, we can then distinguish three kinds of power that are deployed within economic systems: *economic power*, rooted in control over the use of economic resources; *state power*, rooted in control over rule making and rule enforcing over territory; and what I will term *social power*, rooted in the capacity to mobilize people for cooperative, voluntary collective actions. Expressed as a mnemonic slogan, you can get people to do things by bribing them, forcing them, or persuading them. Every complex economic system involves all three forms of power, connected in different ways.

Three ideal types of economic structures—capitalism, statism and socialism—can be differentiated in terms of the dominant form of power controlling economic activity[3]:

- *Capitalism* is an economic structure within which the means of production are privately owned and the allocation and use of resources for different social purposes is accomplished through the exercise of economic power. Investments and the control of production are the result of the exercise of economic power by owners of capital.
- *Statism* is an economic structure within which the means of production are owned by the state and the allocation and use of resources for different social purposes are accomplished through the exercise of state power. State officials control the investment process and production through some sort of state-administrative mechanism.

---

3   This is not meant to be a complete theoretical specification of the differences between these three types of economic structures, but only their differentiation in terms of power relations. For a fuller discussion, see Erik Olin Wright, *Envisioning Real Utopias* (London and New York: Verso, 2010), 11–123.

- *Socialism* is an economic structure within which the means of production are socially owned[4] and the allocation and use of resources for different social purposes are accomplished through the exercise of "social power." In effect this is equivalent to defining socialism as pervasive economic democracy.

These are definitions of ideal types. In the real world, actual economies are complex forms of combination of these three types. They are *hybrids* that vary according to how these different forms of power interact and intermix. To call an economy 'capitalist' is thus a shorthand for a more cumbersome expression such as "an economic hybrid combining capitalist, statist and socialist power relations within which capitalist relations are dominant." The idea of a structural hybrid can be used to analyze any unit of analysis—firms, sectors, regional economies, national economies, even the global economy. The possibility of socialism thus depends on our ability to enlarge and deepen the socialist component of the hybrid and weaken the capitalist and statist components.

This way of thinking about economic systems means abandoning a simple binary notion of capitalism versus socialism. An economic structure can be more or less capitalist, more or less socialist, more or less statist. It is an important, but unresolved, question how stable different kinds of hybrids might be. One traditional Marxian view is that any capitalist hybrid with significant socialist elements would be deeply unstable. The only reasonably stable equilibria, the thinking goes, are ones in which socialism is unequivocally dominant or ones in which capitalism is unequivocally dominant and whatever socialist elements exist fill small niches in the economic system in ways that are functional for capitalism. This is consistent with the organism view of capitalism as a system: a system can be either capitalist or socialist, but not a stable hybrid.

---

4   Social ownership should be distinguished from state ownership. Social ownership of economic resources means that these are owned in common by everyone in a society, and thus everyone has the collective right to decide on the distribution of the net income generated by the use of those resources and the collective right to dispose of those resources. Under conditions of deep and pervasive democracy, state ownership becomes one way of organizing social ownership.

An alternative view is that there may be multiple relatively stable equilibria involving all three economic forms in quite variable combinations, and that it is even possible for there to be an equilibrium involving no clear dominance among them. The extent to which any given configuration could be stable depends upon a complex array of contingent historical and political factors and this makes it impossible to make any general, abstract propositions about what is really possible. My approach is based on the second of these views.

Our task, then, is to clarify the alternative ways in which we can conceptualize the deepening of the socialist component of hybrids. I will refer to this as the problem of the *structural configurations of social empowerment*.

A Visual Vocabulary
In order to explore the problem of deepening the socialist component within hybrid economic systems, it will be useful to represent visually different patterns of interconnection among the three forms of power within economic systems. The visual vocabulary I use for this purpose is illustrated in Figure 1.

The arrows in Figure 1 indicate the direction of influence of one form of power over the use of another; the width of the arrows indicates the strength of this relationship. Thus, in the first illustration in Figure 1, state power is subordinated to social power. This is what is meant conventionally by political democracy as "rule by the people." The expression "rule by the people" does not really mean, rule by the atomized aggregation of the separate individuals of the society taken as isolated persons, but rather, rule by the people collectively organized into voluntary associations in various ways for the purpose of controlling the use of state power, especially through the institutional mechanism of elections. In a democracy, state power is still important—why have a democracy if the state has no capacity to do anything?—but this power is not autonomously exercised by state officials; it is subordinated to social power.

In the second illustration, economic power subordinates social power. The unrestrained use of donations by corporations and the wealthy to fund political parties in the United States would be an example. Political parties still matter—they are the vehicles for selecting state officials who directly exercise state power—but the social power mobilized by political parties is itself subordinated by the exercise of economic power.

Figure 1
Visual Representation of Power Configurations

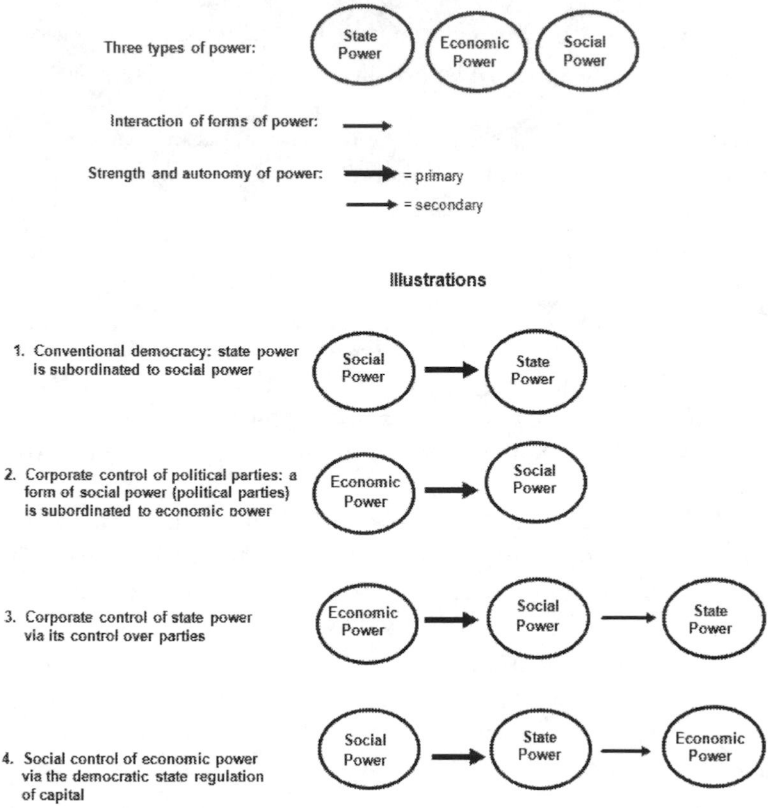

Three types of power:

State Power   Economic Power   Social Power

Interaction of forms of power: ⟶

Strength and autonomy of power: ⟹ = primary
⟶ = secondary

Illustrations

1. Conventional democracy: state power is subordinated to social power

Social Power ⟹ State Power

2. Corporate control of political parties: a form of social power (political parties) is subordinated to economic power

Economic Power ⟹ Social Power

3. Corporate control of state power via its control over parties

Economic Power ⟹ Social Power ⟶ State Power

4. Social control of economic power via the democratic state regulation of capital

Social Power ⟹ State Power ⟶ Economic Power

These configurations can be connected in chains of power relations, as in the third and fourth illustrations. In the first of these, corporate influence over state power occurs through the subordination of political parties to economic power. Finally, in the fourth illustration, social power subordinates economic power through the mediation of state power. This is the ideal of social democracy: the state effectively regulates the behavior of capitalist firms but is itself democratically subordinated to social power.

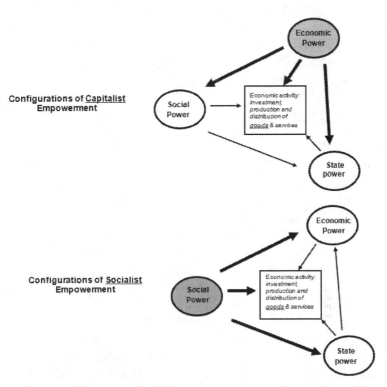

**Figure 2
Aggregate Configurations of
Capitalist Empowerment and Socialist Empowerment**

Figure 2 illustrates the different aggregate configurations of forms of power within a dominant capitalist hybrid economy and within a dominant socialist hybrid economy. In these diagrams, the arrows are all directed towards explaining the control over economic activity: investments, production, and distribution of goods and services. In the picture of capitalist empowerment, both social power and state power are subordinated to economic power in the control over economic activity; in the case of socialist empowerment, both economic power and state power are subordinated to social power.

Configurations of Socialist Empowerment: Pathways for Building a Socialist Hybrid

The basic purpose for which I use these schematic representations is to differentiate salient configurations of social empowerment. Different kinds of progressive policies, institutional innovations and proposals, strategies, and reforms can be located within these various configurations. Seven such configurations are particularly important: (1) statist socialism, (2) social democratic statist regulation, (3) associational democracy, (4) social capitalism, (5) solidarity economy, (6) cooperative market economy, and (7) participatory socialism. I will discuss each of these briefly.

1. *Statist Socialism*

The configuration in Figure 3 corresponds to the classical definition of socialism in which social power controls economic activity via the state. Investment, production, and distribution are directly controlled by the exercise of state power—through, for example, state ownership and control over the commanding heights of the economy—while, at the same time, state power is itself subordinated to social power by being democratically accountable to the people. This is the configuration that was at the core of traditional Marxist ideas of revolutionary socialism. This is not, of course, how the revolutions that occurred in the name of socialism turned out in the twentieth century. Once the power of revolutionary parties was consolidated in the form of the one-party state, "actually existing socialism" became a form of authoritarian statism in which, as illustrated in Figure 4, both social power within civil society and economic power were subordinated to state power.

The experience of authoritarian statism has justifiably lead to great skepticism about the desirability of the centralized state planning

Figure 3
Statist Socialism

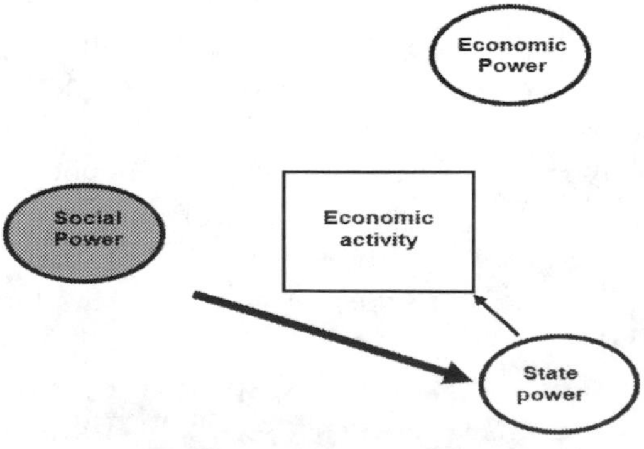

model of socialism. Nevertheless, the power configuration of statist socialism remains an important component of any prospect for transcending capitalism, particularly for large infrastructure projects, systems of public transportation, various kinds of natural monopolies, and for at least the core components of the financial system.

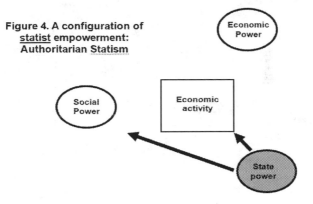

Figure 4. A configuration of statist empowerment: Authoritarian Statism

2. *Social Democratic Statist Regulation*

In the second configuration (Figure 5), social power regulates the economy through the mediation of both state power and economic power. This is a key aspect of social democracy. Capitalist economic power directly controls economic activity—capitalists continue to make investments, hire managers and workers, organize the labor process, etc.—but this power is itself regulated by state power, which is in turn subordinated to social power. Through a transitivity of power relations, this means that social power exerts regulative control over the exercise of economic power. Those forms of regulation of capital that improve working conditions and job security and protect the environment generally reflect this kind of democratic imposition of constraints.

In and of itself, statist regulation of capitalist economic power need not imply significant social empowerment. As in the case of statist socialism, the issue here is the extent and depth to which the power of the state is a genuine expression of democratic empowerment of civil society. In actual capitalist societies, much statist economic regulation is in fact itself subordinated to economic power, as illustrated in Figure 6. In capitalist statist regulation, state power regulates capital but in ways that are systematically responsive to the power of capital itself.

In the United States, the heavy involvement of industry associations in shaping the rules of Federal regulation of airlines, energy, agriculture, and other sectors would be examples. Perhaps even more pervasively, the structural dependency of the state on the capitalist economy underwrites this configuration of power relations.[5]

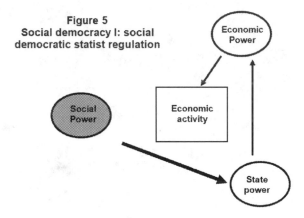

Figure 5
Social democracy I: social democratic statist regulation

Figure 6
A Configuration of <u>Capitalist</u> Empowerment: Capitalist statist regulation

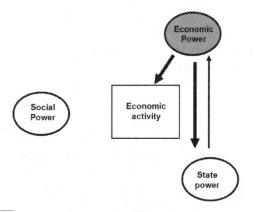

5   Much of the theory of the capitalist character of the capitalist state developed in the late 1960s and 1970s can be interpreted as an attempt to explain how, in spite of the democratic form of the state, much—perhaps most—intervention by the state in the capitalist economy is subordinated to the needs of capital rather than the collective will of the people, and thus, in the present terms, is an expression of economic power rather than social power.

3. *Associational Democracy*

Associational democracy is a term that covers a wide range of institutional devices through which collective associations in civil society directly participate in various kinds of governance activities, usually along with state agencies. The most familiar form of this is probably the tripartite neo-corporatist arrangements in some social democratic societies in which organized labor, employers' associations, and the state bargain over various kinds of economic regulations, especially concerning the labor market and employment relations. Associational democracy can be extended to many other domains, for example watershed councils which bring together civic associations, environmental groups, developers, and state agencies to regulate ecosystems; or health councils involving medical associations, community organizations, and public health officials to plan various aspects of health care. To the extent that the associations involved are internally democratic and representative of interests in civil society, and the decision-making process in which they are engaged is open and deliberative, rather than heavily manipulated by elites and the state, then, associational democracy can contribute to social empowerment.

Figure 7
Social Democracy II: Associational Democracy

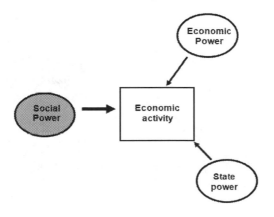

4. *Social Capitalism*

"Social capitalism" is not a standard expression. I use it to describe a power configuration in which secondary associations of civil society, through a variety of mechanisms, directly affect the way economic power is used (Figure 8). The "solidarity funds" in Quebec would be a good example. Unions and other organizations in civil society often manage pension funds for their members. In effect this is collectively controlled capital that can be allocated on various principles. In the Quebec Solidarity Fund, developed by the labor movement initially in the 1980s, investment is used deliberately to protect and create jobs rather than simply to maximize returns for retirement. One way the Solidarity Fund accomplishes this is by directly investing in small and medium enterprises, either through private equity investment or loans. These investments are generally directed at firms that are strongly rooted in the region and satisfy various criteria in a social audit. The Solidarity Fund is also involved in the governance of the firms in which it invests, often by having representation on the board of directors. Solidarity finance thus goes considerably beyond ordinary "socially screened investments" in being much more actively and directly engaged in the project of allocating capital on the basis of social priorities. The idea for stakeholder boards of directors of corporations, in which all stakeholders in the activities of a corporation are represented, also constitutes a form of social capitalism.

Figure 8
Social Economy I: Social Capitalism

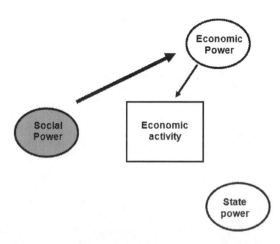

The simple fact that social power has an impact on economic power, however, does not mean that it constitutes a form of social empowerment. In Figure 9, social power affects the exercise of economic power but it does so in a way that is itself subordinated to economic power. An example would be trade associations formed by voluntary cooperation among capitalist firms for the purpose of setting industry standards and in other ways regulating various practices of firms in the sector. This kind of collectively organized self-regulation of sectors constitutes a configuration of capitalist empowerment, not socialist empowerment.

Figure 9
A Configuration of <u>capitalist</u> empowerment:
Corporate capitalist self-regulation

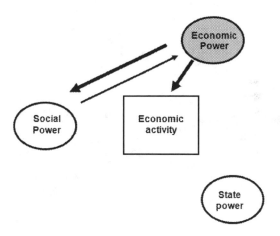

5. *Cooperative Market Economy*

In a fully worker-owned cooperative firm in a capitalist economy the egalitarian principle of one-worker / one-vote of all members of the business means that the power relations within the firm are based on voluntary cooperation and persuasion, not the relative economic power of different people. Jointly they control through democratic means the economic power represented by the capital in the firm. And if individual cooperative firms join together in larger associations of cooperatives—perhaps even a cooperative-of-cooperatives, collectively providing finance, training, and other kinds of support—they begin to transcend the capitalist character of their economic environment by constituting a cooperative market economy (Figure 10). The overarching cooperative in such a market stretches the social character of ownership within individual cooperative enterprises and moves governance more towards a stakeholder model, in which cooperative enterprises are governed by democratic bodies representing all categories of people whose lives are affected by the enterprises' economic activity. The Mondragon Cooperative Corporation would be a partial example. Such firms remain a hybrid economic form, combining capitalist and socialist elements, but a hybrid in which the socialist component has considerable weight.

Figure 10
Social Economy III: Cooperative Market Economy

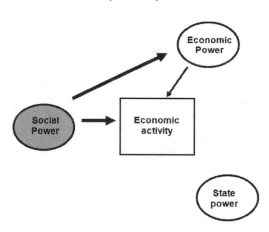

6. The Solidarity Economy

The "solidarity economy" goes beyond other forms of social empowerment by constituting an alternative way of directly organizing economic activity that is distinct from capitalist market production, state organized production, and household production (Figure 11).[6] Its hallmark is production organized by collectivities

---

6   There is no firmly established use of terminology to identify the form of economic organization that I am describing here. Sometimes the terms "social economy" and "solidarity economy" are used more or less interchangeably. Sometimes they are coupled in the expression "the social and solidarity

directly to satisfy human needs not subject to the discipline of profit-maximization or state-technocratic rationality. The state may be involved in funding these collectivities, but it does not directly organize them or their services.[7] The system of child daycare provision in Quebec is a good example. In 2008 parents only paid seven Canadian dollars per day for full-time daycare for preschool children provided by community-based nonprofit daycare center, but provincial government subsidies ensured that providers were paid a living wage. These daycare centers were often organized as "solidarity cooperatives," an organizational form governed by elected representatives of staff, consumers (parents in this case), and community members. Another kind of example is Wikipedia, and other instances of peer-to-peer collaborative network production. Wikipedia produces knowledge and disseminates information outside of markets and without state involvement; the funding comes largely from donations from participants and supporters. In most respects, the system-level proposal for participatory economics as outlined by Robin and Michael Albert can be thought of as a universalization of the solidarity economy configuration to an entire economy.

---

economy." Generally it seems that the term social economy is used as a broader, more heterogeneous umbrella term than solidarity economy, although both are meant to identify more egalitarian, socially oriented forms of economic life than capitalism. Here I will use the term "solidarity economy" to define the form of social economy in which social power—i.e. voluntary cooperation for collective purposes—plays the most direct and unmediated role in organizing economic activity, and use the term social economy as broader rubric for ways in which social power shapes economic activity without the direct mediation of the state.

7   Of course, in a sense the state is always involved in all economic activities insofar as it enforces rules of the game, imposes taxes, etc. The issue here is that in the solidarity economy the state operates in a relatively passive way in the background rather than directly organizing economic activity or regulating economic power. Because the state is on the sidelines, political conservatives and libertarians are often relatively enthusiastic about certain kinds of solidarity economy initiatives (although they don't use the term), particularly when these activities are anchored in religious communities or other socially conservative organizations. When the solidarity economy embodies ideals of economic democracy and egalitarian participation, the initiatives pose a bigger challenge to free market ideologies.

Figure 11
Social Economy III: The solidarity economy

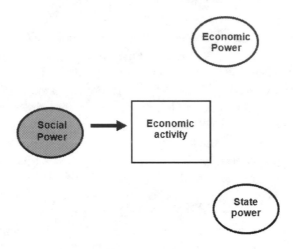

7. Participatory Socialism

The final configuration of social empowerment combines the solidarity economy and statist socialism: the state and civil society jointly organize and control various kinds of production of goods and services (Figure 12). In participatory socialism the role of the state is more pervasive than in the pure social economy. The state does not simply provide funding and set the parameters; it is also, in various ways, directly involved in the organization and production of the economic activity. On the other hand, participatory socialism is also different from statist socialism, for here social power plays a role not simply through the ordinary channels of democratic control of state policies, but directly inside the productive activities themselves. An example is the participatory budget in urban government. Since these budgets constitute allocations of resources to produce infrastructure to meet human needs, they should be treated as an aspect of economic activity, and thus participatory budgets are not simply a form of democratic participation in the state, but of a participatory socialist economy.

The Seven Configurations Together

As summarized in Figure 13, the different configurations of social empowerment we have been examining can be clustered into three

Figure 12
Participatory Socialism

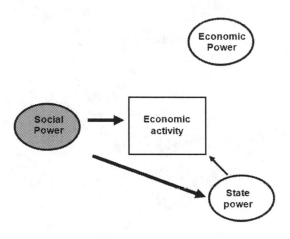

broad groups, each corresponding to different political traditions of socio-economic transformation: a socialist cluster, a social economy cluster, and a social democratic cluster. These different clusters vary in the role they accord to the state and the extent to which they attempt to subordinate rather than bypass capitalist economic power. What all of the configurations have in common is the idea of democratization of power over economic life by subordinating both economic power and state power to social power, power rooted in voluntary cooperation for collective action. Of course, the ideal of socialism involves much more than this. Equality and social justice are also core traditional socialist values, to which environmental sustainability should be added today. What this model of socialism stresses, however, is that the realization of all these values depends upon the transformation of the power relations over economic activity, in terms of the ways social power is both directly involved in shaping economic activity and indirectly through the democratization of the state.

What about Markets?
The framework elaborated above says almost nothing explicitly about markets. To be sure, the dominance of economic power in capitalism rests in significant ways on the centrality of markets as the organizing

Figure 13
Combined configurations of social empowerment

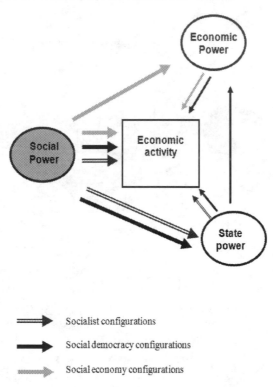

Socialist configurations

Social democracy configurations

Social economy configurations

principle for the exchange of private property rights. And it is certainly the case that the subordination of economic power to social power—either directly or indirectly via the state—would entail pervasive democratic regulation of markets far beyond the kinds of constraints on markets within capitalism.[8] But the framework itself does not imply either the possibility or desirability of abolishing markets. The precise scope of market transactions and market-like

8   Markets, of course, are always regulated in one way or another, both by the state and by other mechanisms (including norms, associational regulation by capitalists, and what sociologists call social embeddedness). The "free" market in the sense fantasized by many defenders of capitalism is a myth. But the character and depth of regulation in a socialist economy, and especially the purposes and interests served by regulation, would go far beyond anything that occurs within capitalism.

processes relative to democratically planned allocations of resources depends on the practical trade-offs people face under conditions of broad democratic power over the economy and the results of the continual process of experimentation with alternative solutions to these trade-offs.

Stating the problem of markets in this way implies that I do not see market transactions as such as intrinsically undesirable. What is undesirable are two things that are generally strongly linked to markets: first, the ways in which markets can enable people and organizations with specific kinds of power to gain advantages over others, and second, the way markets, *if inadequately regulated*, generate all sorts of destructive externalities and harms on people. But if those problems are minimized through various mechanisms, then the sheer fact of buyers and sellers of goods and services agreeing to exchange things at a mutually agreed-upon price is not, in and of itself, objectionable.

This is the issue that is most in contention in this dialogue with Robin. Both Robin and I share a commitment to the values of democracy and equality, and both of us understand these values in similarly radical ways. We both understand democracy as an ideal in which people should be able to participate in decisions to the extent that they are affected by those decisions. And we both see equality as demanding an economic system that both meets people's basic needs to live a flourishing life and allocates rewards above this level on the basis of the burdens people take on in their work (or "effort" in Robin's usual formulation).[9] Both of these values are generally violated by the unfettered operation of market processes: markets systematically generate unjust inequalities and also, inherently violate democratic principles by enabling people to engage in exchange without regard to social costs. For these reasons, Robin argues that in an

---

9 The central moral idea is that rewards should be proportional to burden or sacrifice. Sometimes people use the term effort in precisely this way, as something unpleasant, a "disutility" of labor to use the economist's expression. But sometimes effort simply reflects the level of energy and enthusiasm a person expends in a task, which may not at all imply sacrifice. For certain kinds of tasks expending a great deal of effort is more intrinsically rewarding than doing the task in a less intense way. It is for this reason that I prefer the expressions burden or sacrifice in talking about fair rewards.

ideal economy—an economy that fully realizes democratic and egalitarian values—markets would disappear and be replaced by something like participatory planning. In terms of my categories of configurations of social empowerment, his model for an alternative economy beyond capitalism would fall under the single structural configuration of social empowerment that I identify as the solidarity economy (Figure 11).[10]

Since I share these basic values and also acknowledge that markets tend to generate these moral deficits, why then do I take the position that in a democratic egalitarian economy beyond capitalism there is likely to be a significant role for markets? There are two main issues in play here.

The first issue concerns the complex trade-offs involved in the actual process of designing and implementing institutional solutions to socio-economic problems. In transcending a system as complex as capitalism, there will necessarily be many trade-offs among competing values, and in some settings and contexts, markets may play a positive role in resolving these difficulties. This is not simply the case for the "transition problem"—how to move from capitalism to a democratic-egalitarian alternative—but also in the institutional configuration of the destination itself. Markets, in one form or another, are likely to be a desirable part of solutions to some of the design problems. To take a fairly simple example, consider the problem of second-hand goods, things people have already purchased and no longer want. One institutional solution is simply allowing people to sell these to whomever wants them at whatever price the parties agree to; another would be to submit proposals for what to do with such goods to the consumption planning process. In a world in which people are ecologically conscious about waste, a market in second-hand goods might be quite a significant market and account for a sizable part of total consumption. What is the optimal way of organizing the distribution of second-hand goods? A market solution might simply be better than

---

10   In Figure 11 the solidarity economy is identified as the direct, unmediated subordination of economic activities to social power. The processes of participatory planning outlined by Robin can be viewed as the mechanisms embodied in the arrow between social power and economic activities.

participatory planning for the allocation of second-hand goods consumption—less hassle, quicker, fewer transaction costs, etc. Or consider a quite different kind of example: the allocation of tickets and seats in the performing arts. Getting tickets to a particular performance matters much more to some people than to others, as does getting the best seats. As long as the underlying income structure is just by egalitarian standards, I don't see any reason why the price of theatre tickets shouldn't be a simple reflection of what people are willing to pay for better and worse seats for a given production. This does not mean, of course, that the performers and staff in a theatre collective would receive as income the full price of what people are willing to pay for tickets in the market, for this would violate the fair rewards principle. Taxation of ticket-generated income could prevent that from happening. But having ticket and seat prices adjust to "market demand" could still be the optimal way of distributing them.[11] These are just two examples of situations in which market solutions to institutional design problems may be optimal; many other examples can easily be given.

The second issue for why markets may be a significant design element in the best possible real utopian alternative to capitalism (and not simply in the transition) concerns the weight of market-like mechanisms within any effective planning process. I don't want to get into an arcane definitional discussion here about what counts as a market or not, but the basic point is fairly straightforward. In Robin's model of a democratic-egalitarian economic system without markets, allocations of resources to alternative production processes and the prices for the outputs are initially determined through an iterated participatory planning process that links consumption planning and

---

11   The performing arts are, of course, a fairly special case, but it can be considered an instance of a more general kind of problem: the pricing of services that vary in their desirability (or quality) and in which it is not possible to simply produce more in response to demand. Seats in athletic events of a popular team have this character, but the extent of the demand for seats will depend on the success of the team. Should tickets be available by lottery? Should a secondary market be allowed? Restaurants have somewhat this character also. Again, if the background conditions of income distribution are fair, then the best solution to these problems might well be to allow a regulated market to function where access is rationed by the willingness of people to pay premium prices for the best seats and most popular events.

production planning. There are two critical features of this process that could, in practice, assume a very market-like character. First, in the actual execution of these plans, there are what Robin terms "adjustments." What is unspecified—because it is really unspecifiable in advance—is the magnitude of these adjustments relative to the initial allocations, and what role market-like processes of demand and supply play in shaping the prices in these adjustments. If these adjustments are fairly large and include things like "clearance sales" in which prices drop significantly to clear inventory, then the adjustment part of the overall allocation and pricing process could look very much like a market process. Second, in the initial iterated planning process, consumers submit proposed consumption plans for the year ahead. If, in practice, nearly everyone simply submits the "default" plan of consuming the same pattern they actually did in the previous year (i.e. what they consumed after the previous year's adjustments), then in effect the initial input from consumers into the planning process also looks very much like the information a market provides producers: producers already know, without the additional input of "plans" from consumers, what the total pattern of consumption was the previous year.

My basic point here is that markets and market-like arrangements within the planning process are likely to be elements of any complex democratically organized economic system because the people living in those systems will see these arrangements as the simplest and most effective way of dealing with certain specific problems. Of course, none of these issues in the design of a democratic-egalitarian economy implies that the market elements in the system function in the same way as in a system without participatory planning. The planning process itself changes the ramifications of these market-like elements.

In the end, therefore, the issue is not really planning versus markets, but the specific articulation of planning mechanisms and market mechanisms in shaping the way allocations for the production and distribution of different kinds of goods and services occur. At this point in history, when we are so far from the realization of a world in which economic democracy has been realized in any form, we cannot reasonably predict what people would choose (or even prescribe what they *should* choose) if they had the power to do so. How much markets and market-like processes will be part of the institutional configuration for stably realising democratic-egalitarian principles will depend on a range of practical issues, many of which cannot be anticipated in advance.

Real Utopias and Transformation

Transforming capitalism in a socialist direction means democratizing the economy through the seven configurations summarized in Figure 13. In this process the economic structure remains a hybrid—combining capitalist, statist, and socialist practices and relations—but the socialist dimension gains weight and centrality. Extending and deepening social power in any one of these configurations may be quite compatible with maintaining the dominance of capitalism, but *if* it is possible to increase social power within all of these configurations, the cumulative effect could be a qualitative transformation in which socialism becomes the dominant form of relations within a complex economic hybrid, subordinating both capitalism and statism within democratized power relations.

This, of course, is a very big "if." Skepticism towards socialism at the beginning of the twenty-first century is at least as much about the prospects of challenging the dominance of capitalist relations as it is in the viability of alternative institutions if they could be created. The power of capital seems so massive that if ever social power seemed to threaten the dominance of capitalism, it would be relentlessly attacked and undermined. Real progress in advancing the project of democratizing the economy through these configurations seems impossible so long as capitalism is dominant. For this reason, radical anti-capitalists have often felt that decisively breaking the power of capital was a precondition for significant movement towards socialism rather than mainly a consequence of such movement.

Marx had an elegant solution to this problem. He believed that in the long run, capitalism destroyed its own conditions of existence: the laws of motion and contradictions of capitalism ultimately make capitalism an increasingly fragile and vulnerable system in which the ability of the ruling class and its political allies to block transformation becomes progressively weaker over time. Eventually capitalism has so weakened its own conditions of existence that it becomes overthrowable. This was a strong prediction, not simply a weak claim about future possibilities.[12] This doesn't solve the problem of exactly how to build the emancipatory alternative to capitalism, but at least it makes the problem of overcoming the obstacles of existing power relations much less daunting in the long run.

Relatively few people today—even those who still work within the Marxist tradition—feel confident that capitalism will destroy itself. Capitalism may be crisis ridden and cause great suffering in the world, but it also has enormous resilience and capacity to effectively block alternatives. The problem of its transformation, at least in the developed world, therefore cannot be treated as mainly the problem of "seizing the time" when capitalism through its own contradictions becomes so weak and chaotic that it is vulnerable to being overthrown. Rather, the problem of transformation requires understanding the ways in which *strategies* of transformation have some prospect in the long term of eroding capitalist power relations and building up socialist alternatives.

Three strategic logics of transformation have characterized the history of anti-capitalist struggle. I refer to these as ruptural, interstitial, and symbiotic strategies:

- *Ruptural* transformations envision creating new emancipatory institutions through a sharp break with existing institutions and social structures. The central image is very much that of a war in which ultimately victory depends on the decisive defeat of the enemy in a direct confrontation. The result of victory is a radical disjuncture in which existing institutions are destroyed and new ones built in a fairly rapid way. In most versions, this revolutionary scenario involves seizing state power, rapidly transforming state structures and then using these new

---

12 While there is considerable debate on this matter, I think Marx was largely a determinist about the ultimate demise of capitalism, even if he was not a determinist about the process of actually constructing socialism. Capitalism could not, he believed, survive indefinitely in the face of the inevitable intensification of the contradictions generated by its laws of motion. This does not mean that the overthrow of capitalism must wait until the literal collapse of capitalism, but it does mean that it progressively becomes more vulnerable to overthrow as its sustainability becomes ever more fragile. For my assessment of this argument, see Erik Olin Wright, Chapter 4 in *Envisioning Real Utopias* (London and New York: Verso, 2010)

apparatuses of state power to destroy the power of the dominant class within the economy.

- *Interstitial* transformations seek to build new forms of social empowerment in the niches and margins of capitalist society where this is possible, often where they do not seem to pose any immediate threat to dominant classes and elites. Prodhoun's vision of building a cooperative alternative to capitalism within capitalism itself is a nineteenth-century version of this perspective. The many experiments in the social economy today are also examples. The central theoretical idea is that building alternatives on the ground in whatever spaces are possible both serves a critical ideological function of showing that alternative ways of working and living are possible, and potentially erodes the constraints on the spaces themselves.[13]

- *Symbiotic* transformations involve strategies that use the state to extend and deepen the institutional forms of social empowerment in ways which also solve certain practical problems faced by dominant classes and elites. The basic idea here is that there are multiple institutional equilibria within capitalism, all of which are functionally *compatible* with capitalism (i.e. they contribute to solving problems of capitalist reproduction), but some of which are better for capitalists than others and some of which involve more social empowerment than others. A symbiotic transformation is one that seeks to expand social empowerment while still achieving an institutional configuration that contributes to an adequately well-functioning capitalism. This is what in the 1970s was called "non-reformist reforms"—reforms that simultaneously make life better within the existing economic system and expand the potential for future advances of democratic power. It is also reflected in a variety of forms of civic activism in which social movements, local leaders and city governments collaborate in ways that both enhance democracy and solve practical problems.

---

13   The idea of interstitial transformation resonates with various strands of nonviolent activism in which people are exhorted (in words apocryphally attributed to Gandhi) to "be the change you want to see in the world." The difference is that interstitial transformation involves collectively building new institutions embodying the kind of changed world you want, not just individually behaving in a dignified, value-affirming way.

All three of these strategic logics have historically had a place within anti-capitalist social movements and politics. Ruptural strategies are most closely associated with revolutionary socialism and communism, interstitial strategies with some strands of anarchism, and symbiotic strategies with social democracy. It is easy to raise objections to each of them. Ruptural strategies have a grandiose, romantic appeal to critics of capitalism, but the historical record is pretty dismal. There are no cases in which socialism as defined here—a deeply democratic and egalitarian organization of power relations within an economy—has been a robust result of a ruptural strategy of transformation of capitalism. Ruptural strategies seem in practice more prone to result in authoritarian statism than democratic socialism. Interstitial strategies may produce improvements in the lives of people and pockets of more democratic-egalitarian practices, but they also have nowhere succeeded in significantly eroding capitalist power relations. As for symbiotic strategies, in the most successful instances of social democracy, they have certainly resulted in a more humane capitalism—with less poverty, less inequality, and less insecurity—but they have done so in ways which stabilize capitalism and leave intact the core powers of capital. Any advance of symbiotic strategies historically that appeared to potentially threaten those core powers was massively resisted by capital. The reaction of Swedish capitalists to proposals for serious union involvement in control over investment in the late 1970s is one of the best-known examples. These are all reasonable objections. Taken together they suggest to many people that transcending capitalism through some kind of long-term coherent *strategy* is simply not possible.

Pessimism is intellectually easy, perhaps even intellectually lazy. It often reflects a simple extrapolation of past experience into the future. Our theories of the future, however, are far too weak to really make confident claims that we know what *can't* happen. The appropriate orientation towards strategies of social transformation, therefore, is to do things now which put us in the best position to do more later by working to create those institutions and structures that increase, rather than decrease, the prospects of taking advantage of whatever historical opportunities emerge. Building real utopias can both prefigure more comprehensive alternatives and move us in the direction of those alternatives.

In these terms, I think the best prospect for the future in developed capitalist countries is a strategic orientation mainly organized around the interplay of interstitial and symbiotic strategies, with perhaps periodic episodes involving elements of ruptural strategy. Through interstitial strategies, activists and communities can build and strengthen real utopian economic institutions embodying democratic-egalitarian principles where this is possible. Symbiotic strategies through the state can help open up greater space and support for these interstitial innovations. The interplay between interstitial and symbiotic strategies could then create a trajectory of deepening socialist elements within the hybrid capitalist economic ecosystem.

Worker cooperatives are a good example. Under existing conditions, worker cooperatives face serious obstacles to becoming a significant component of market economies: credit markets are skeptical of worker-owned firms; risk-averse workers are reluctant to sink their savings in a venture that has low probability of success; cooperatives face supply chains in which, because of scale, they face higher costs than capitalist corporate rivals; and so on. Symbiotic strategies directed at public policy could address all of these issues. Given the potential for worker-owned cooperatives to help solve problems of unemployment, deteriorating tax bases, and unstable communities, new rules of the game to support cooperatives could gain political traction. Even within the logic of market economies, the positive externalities of worker cooperatives provide a justification for public subsidies and insurance schemes to increase their viability. Such policies could, over time, expand the weight of a cooperative market economy within the broader capitalist economic hybrid.

Many other real utopian institutions and innovations could contribute to deepening the forms of social empowerment over economic life. Some of these can take place with little or no state involvement; others would be greatly enhanced by various kinds of state support. Here are a few additional examples:[14]

- Peer-to-peer collaborative production: Wikipedia, open-source software

---

14 Most of these are discussed at length in Wright, chapters 6 and 7 in *Envisioning Real Utopias*.

- Urban agriculture with community land trusts
- Community-owned fab labs for advanced customized small-batch cooperative manufacturing
- Open-access intellectual property: creative commons, copyleft, open source pharmaceuticals, free downloadable blueprints for 3-D printing
- Free publicly provided goods/services: libraries, public transport
- Unconditional basic income
- Policy juries and "randomocracy"
- Eco-villages and transition towns

Such a combination of symbiotic and interstitial strategies does not imply that the process of transformation could ever follow a smooth path of enlightened cooperation between conflicting class forces. What is ultimately at stake here is a transformation of the core power relations of capitalism, and this does ultimately threaten the interests of capitalists. While elites may become resigned to a diminution of power, they are unlikely to gracefully embrace the prospects. While symbiotic transformations help solve problems within capitalism, they often are not optimal for elites and are thus resisted. This means that a key element of ruptural strategies—confrontations between opposing organized social forces in which there are winners and losers—will be a part of any plausible trajectory of sustainable social empowerment. The purpose of such confrontations, however, is not a systemic rupture with capitalist dominance, but rather creating more space for the interplay of interstitial and symbiotic strategies.

Conclusion

The framework proposed here for a socialism rooted in social empowerment involves a commitment to institutional pluralism and heterogeneity. Instead of a unitary institutional design for transcending capitalism, the configurations of social empowerment open up space for a wide diversity of institutional forms. Worker cooperatives and local social economy projects, state-run banks and enterprises, social democratic regulation of private corporations, solidarity finance, and participatory budgeting all potentially undermine the dominance of capitalism and increase the weight of social power within the hybrid economic ecosystem. These diverse forms all increase social power, but they do not point to an integrated, comprehensive system driven by a single institutional design principle of the sort proposed by Robin in his analysis of participatory economics.

The institutional pluralism of the destination also suggests strategic pluralism in the practices of transformation. Within some of these configurations, to strengthen social power requires access to state power. But other configurations can be advanced even without state power. This is especially true for the social economy initiatives— worker cooperatives, community-based urban agriculture, solidarity finance, community land trusts, etc. Activists on the left, especially those on the radical left, have often regarded these kinds of locally-oriented, community-based initiatives as not being very "political," since they do not always involve direct confrontation with political power. This is a narrow view of politics. Interstitial strategies to create real utopias involve showing that another world is possible by building it in the spaces available, and then pushing against the state and public policy to expand those spaces. For many people these kinds of interstitial initiatives also have the advantage of generating immediate, tangible results in which each person's contribution clearly matters. A vision of emancipatory alternatives that is anchored in the multidimensional and multiscalar problem of deepening democracy can encompass this wide range of strategies and projects of transformation.

CHAPTER 5

Breaking with Capitalism

Robin Hahnel

In "Socialism and Real Utopias" Erik comments on how to think about systemic alternatives, argues that markets can play a positive role in a fully desirable economy, and discusses transition strategy. Below I comment briefly on questions of methodology and social theory before going on to discuss markets at greater length. After identifying large areas of agreement with only minor disagreements with regard to transition strategy, I close with some personal observations about the response to our model of a participatory economy over the past twenty years.

Thinking about Systemic Alternatives

Both Erik and I have contributed to a vast literature on "social theory."[1] All either of us can hope to do in this dialogue is briefly discuss a few insights we believe are particularly relevant.

1. Erik distinguishes between an "organism" vs. "ecological" view of human societies, and observes that "the idea of real utopias as a way of transforming a society is more in line with the ecosystems view" where transformation results from introducing "an alien

---

1   As an alternative to Marxist historical materialism, I helped develop a social theory known as "complimentary holism," which purports to provide a more realistic and useful framework for thinking about relations between the "human center" and "institutional boundary" of societies, the political, kinship, community, and economic "spheres of social life"; and the conscious and unconscious forces that operate to stabilize and destabilize societies. This is not the place for Erik or me to explain our full thoughts on social theory. Readers interested in mine should see Michael Albert and Robin Hahnel *Marxism and Socialist Theory* (Boston: South End Press, 1981); Hahnel et al., *Liberating Theory* (Boston: South End Press, 1986); and Hahnel, Chapter 1 in *The ABCs of Political Economy: A Modern Approach,* 2nd edition (London: Pluto Press, 2014).

species which finds a niche and then gradually increases, potentially even displacing certain other species."

The problem with the "society as ecological system" metaphor is that there are cases where the "society as organic system" metaphor is more apt. For example, what if an "alien species" of socially empowering institutions we seek to introduce into a capitalist economy cannot survive, or if survival requires becoming co-opted? A "pure cooperativist" strategy for social change is to introduce more and more "alien" cooperative "species" into capitalism until "native" private enterprise "species" are all replaced. But there are many who have argued that simply introducing more cooperatives into capitalism cannot achieve "system change" precisely because they will either fail or become co-opted.

I do not bring this up because I believe Erik and I actually disagree about cooperatives. We both believe they can play a positive role as *one part* of a successful transition strategy, while neither of us thinks "one, two, many cooperatives" can be a successful strategy all by itself. My point is simply that the analogy Erik offers does not settle any of the issues that—to use Erik's words—"rupturalists," "interstitialists," and "symbioticists" argue over. It is merely an analogy that inclines one to think more along interstitial and symbiotic lines, which is Erik's inclination.

2. Erik distinguishes between "ameliorative reforms"—which, to his credit, he argues deserve our full support because they are beneficial even though they are not "transformative"—and "real utopian transformations"—which he claims are both beneficial in the here and now and transformative. Elsewhere I have angered most of my closest radical friends by disputing that "non-reformist reforms" can be meaningfully distinguished from "reformist reforms."[2] In brief, I

---

2 See "The Myth of Non-reformist Reforms," in *Economic Justice and Democracy: From Competition to Cooperation* (NY: Routledge, 2005), 154–6. To be blunt, I think the idea of "non-reformist reforms" is intellectually vacuous, but often a socially useful psychological crutch for radicals. All too often those who want system change find it difficult to motivate themselves to participate whole heartedly in reform campaigns even though they should. However, if radicals convince themselves it is a "non-reformist reform" they have less trouble motivating themselves to pitch in. Apparently radicals, like most humans, must sometimes resort to "necessary illusions" to motivate themselves to do what they should. In which case, what I probably should say to my radical comrades is: if

argue that it is a mistake to think that the key to fighting for reforms in ways that undermines the system lies in picking a particular kind of reform, i.e. choosing reforms that are somehow particularly deadly silver bullets. I argue instead that the key is how we go about waging the fight for whatever reform we are working for, rather than what the particular reform happens to be.

Any successful reform campaign will make capitalism less harmful to some extent. There is no way around this, and even if there were such a thing as a non-reformist reform, it would not change this fact. However, just because every reform success makes capitalism less harmful need not prolong the life of capitalism—although it might, and this is something I argue anti-capitalists must learn to accept without regret.[3] But if winning a reform further empowers those who challenged the status quo, if it fortifies emancipating institutions and weakens oppressive institutions, if it whets reformers' appetite for more economic democracy, more economic justice, and more environmental protection than capitalism can provide, then a successful reform campaign can also help lead to system change. In sum, *any* reform can be fought for in ways that diminish the chances of further gains, and *any* reform can be fought for in ways that make further progress more likely.

3. Erik compares trying to "create a detailed account of the critical institutions of an alternative system," to limiting ourselves to "enunciate the basic values that animate the search for alternatives and the core principles of institutional design," and argues that while "both of these strategies have value" he is more inclined to the second approach. I would add one consideration he fails to mention when evaluating the pros and cons of the two approaches.

The second approach runs a greater risk of permitting people to dream about things that are actually not possible. Because it keeps discussion at the level of "values," and tolerates imprecision about how something would actually be done, it can permit people to

---

labeling a reform "non-reformist" helps motivate you to get off the side line and participate whole heartedly, be my guest!

3   Those who foolishly root for worsening conditions because they believe it will drive people to rebel more quickly are prime examples of radicals who have failed to learn this important lesson. Those who capitalism victimizes learn quickly to despise any who display this attitude, as they should.

continue to hold onto views that are self-contradictory. For example, limiting discussion to basic values can delude people into thinking that markets are compatible with economic justice and democracy, or that central planning is compatible with worker self-management. Requiring visionaries to spell out exactly how they propose decisions be made can serve as an important bulwark against this kind of self-deception, which I believe has been all too common on the left. It is also the only way I know to convince people that this time anti-capitalists really do have a better idea how to make dreams come true, because everyone knows that last time we did not.

A Social System

Since he does not discuss political, cultural, or kinship systems, Erik is only talking about economic systems, not entire social systems, when he talks of three traditional "ideal types" and seven non-traditional ideal types. As a long-time comparative economic systems professor, I classify economic systems differently, based on who owns productive assets, who manages production processes, and how any division of labor is coordinated.[4] But in the interest of brevity, let me comment briefly on how Erik puts his frameworks to use.

Erik points out that most real-world economies are hybrids in the sense that they contain elements from more than one ideal type. Using his three-system framework he suggests: "The possibility of socialism thus depends on our ability to enlarge and deepen the socialist component of the hybrid and weaken the capitalist and statist components. This way of thinking about economic systems means abandoning a simple binary notion of capitalism versus social-ism." Sometimes this is useful, but it ignores thorny problems about compatibility, and contains an implicit bias toward an incremental approach to social change.

---

4 It is rather straightforward to classify all the economic "models" in the literature as different combinations of a few possible institutional choices in each of the three areas—ownership, management, and coordination of any division of labor. For example, the model of a participatory economy can be classified as: social ownership (not private ownership), worker self-managed (not "other" directed), with a particular democratic planning procedure to coordinate a significant division of labor (rather than leaving coordination of a significant division of labor to markets, or an authoritarian planning procedure, or minimizing the division of labor by making communities largely self-sufficient.)

For example, the Chavez government chose to leave the private and state sectors of the Venezuelan economy largely in place, and concentrate instead on building a new sector they call "the social economy" comprised of worker-owned cooperatives, neighborhood clinics, food stores, educational "misiones," municipal assemblies, and most recently, communal councils. In that context Erik's approach makes all the sense in the world. In Venezuela socialism depended on their "ability to enlarge and deepen" the new social economy and reduce the capitalist and state sectors of the old economy. But Erik's framework does not help us understand how and why it may be unrealistic to expect people to behave in socially responsible ways in the social economy while others are permitted to profit from socially irresponsible behavior in the capitalist sector, or when society's most valuable resources, in the case of Venezuelan oil, are reserved for the state sector. Incrementalism also has no answers for situations where one must either make a qualitative change or accept eventual re-stabilization back to the old status quo. An entirely incremental strategy implicitly assumes that no such bridges will ever present themselves.

However, let me be clear: Right now in the United States, where we are nowhere near having sufficient popular support for change to a highly democratic economic system, and where radicals and reformers must both become much stronger in a number of areas, like Erik, I am an unapologetic incrementalist and think rupturalist talk is premature. However, let me flag two situations where incremental strategies become problematic and I would not support them.

1. Different economic systems rely on different ways to motivate people. At some point I believe Venezuela will have to choose between motivating people through greed and fear—as they do in their private sector—ordering people around—as they do in their state sector—and motivating people by letting them decide what they want to do as long as it is socially responsible, and rewarding people according to their work efforts—as they are trying to do in their "social economy." In other words, once the social economy has proved its superiority to a majority of Venezuelans, because their incentive systems are not only different but also contradictory, I think it would be a mistake not to extend the social economy system to the entire economy in a non-incremental way.

2. Those who benefit from the status quo can become very aggressive when they feel their privileges slipping away. Failure to take

decisive action to defend our right to continue making progress that a majority supports is a recipe for disaster. In cases where privileged economic elites refuse to accept the will of the majority, the best decisive action is often to strip them of their power by making a dramatic and qualitative change in how the economic system functions. Failure to disarm defeated enemies is poor military strategy.

I am also concerned that Erik may render the useful notions of "stability" and "instability" vacuous. He writes:

> One . . . view is that any capitalist hybrid with significant socialist elements would be deeply unstable. The only reasonably stable equilibria, the thinking goes, are ones in which socialism is unequivocally dominant or ones in which capitalism is unequivocally dominant . . . An alternative view is that there may be multiple relatively stable equilibria involving all three economic forms in quite variable combinations . . . The arguments of this paper are based on the second of these views.

If this is my choice, then I am more inclined to the first view that Erik rejects. For example, to expect a mixture of one-third capitalism, one-third statism, and one-third socialism to be as stable as a mix of nine-tenths capitalism, one-twentieth statism, and one-twentieth socialism seems to me farfetched. As a general rule, I think the more hybrid a system is the less stable it is likely to be. Of course a strongly hybrid system could be poised on a knife edge for quite some time, just as a largely pure system might be transformed. But there is a reason that hybridization breeds instability, and it is the same reason that incrementalism does not always work.

Any economic system relies on people to think and behave in particular ways. Different economic systems require people to think and behave in different ways. The kind of humans capitalism requires, and the kind of humans we tend to become when we play our appointed roles under capitalist institutions, are different from the kind of humans socialism requires, and participation in socialist institutions tends to create. In other words, when we choose to use particular institutions to organize and govern our economic activities we are also choosing to some extent what kind of people we want to become. And this is why hybrids are generally less stable. In a capitalist-socialist hybrid, when capitalist institutions mold people to better conform with the roles they must play for the capitalist part to function effectively and smoothly, they rob the socialist part of the kind of personnel needed to play the roles required for the socialist part to function effectively and smoothly. Or, to put it differently, we humans find it difficult to serve two different masters.

But let me conclude this part on a note of agreement. Erik writes:

> Relatively few people today—even those who still work within the Marxist tradition—feel confident that capitalism will destroy itself. Capitalism may be crisis ridden and cause great suffering in the world, but it also has an enormous capacity to effectively block alternatives. The problem of its transformation, at least in the developed world, therefore cannot be treated as mainly the problem of 'seizing the time' when capitalism through its own contradictions becomes so weak and chaotic that it is vulnerable to being overthrown. Rather, the problem of transformation requires understanding the ways in which *strategies* of transformation have some prospect in the long term of eroding capitalist power relations and building up socialist alternatives.

I could not agree more. Disavowing theories that capitalism is programmed to self-destruct due to internal contradictions as ill conceived and untrue is extremely important if we are to have a realistic view of the nature of the task before us.[5]

---

5   As an aside, I think there is a link between the view of capitalism as doomed by internal contradictions—which Erik and I both reject—and the notion of "non-reformist reforms" that has gone unnoticed. Aside from the crucial question of how reforms are fought for, if all reforms improve outcomes there are only two ways a reform, itself, could be "non-reformist." Either it "heightens" some internal contradiction and thereby undermines the system, or it "prefigures" a solution that is part of a post-capitalist system. I think any who believes in non-reformist reforms for the first reason is chasing a myth. On the other hand, I think the second strategic idea makes all the sense in the world. My argument for the importance of creating real-world examples of "imperfect experiments in equitable cooperation" that others frequently call "prefigurative" organizing, in combination with reform organizing, is discussed further below. I think Erik and I agree on this and that when he distinguishes between "ameliorative reforms" and "real utopian transformations" he is talking about what I call "reform organizing" as distinct from building real-world "experiments in equitable cooperation."

What about Markets?

Points of Agreement

I agree with Erik that markets are "the issue that is most in contention in this dialogue." I also think he is correct that we do not disagree about markets because we disagree about what economic democracy and economic justice mean. As Erik points out: "Both Robin and I . . . understand democracy as an ideal in which people should be able to participate in decisions to the extent that they are affected by those decisions. And we both see equality as demanding an economic system that both meets people's basic needs to live a flourishing life and allocates rewards above this level on the basis of the burdens people take on in their work." This is important because most often people who disagree about markets do so because they disagree about what economic justice and democracy require.

I also endorse Erik's summary of my position:

> Both of these values are generally violated by the unfettered oper-
> ation of market processes: markets systematically generate unjust
> inequalities and also, inherently violate democratic principles by
> enabling people to engage in exchange without regard to social
> costs. For these reasons, Robin argues that in an ideal economy—
> an economy that fully realizes democratic and egalitarian
> values—markets would disappear and be replaced by something
> like participatory planning.

This is what I mean when I call myself a market "abolitionist." In contrast, Erik is "agnostic" with regard to markets, whose use he argues should depend on "practical trade-offs," not just during transition but also "in the institutional configuration of the destination itself."

To be clear, I have never questioned whether or not markets will continue to play a role during a transition to a desirable economic future—which seems obvious to me—nor whether during transition we should often participate in campaigns to "tame" markets to reduce their negative consequences—which also seems obvious to me. So if we do not disagree about goals, and we are not talking about markets and the need to tame them during transition, why do we disagree about whether there is a place for markets in a truly desirable economy? As I said in the first round of this dialogue, the case against markets logically consists of two parts: How bad are markets? And, is there a more desirable alternative that is feasible? I have presented my case for what I believe is a feasible and desirable alternative. I will now outline the case for why we should embrace the desirable alternative that is feasible and eventually eliminate markets altogether.

The Dispassionate Case Against Markets

Efficiency: It is well known among professional economists that markets allocate resources inefficiently when they are out of equilibrium, when they are non-competitive, and when there are external effects. When the fundamental theorem of welfare economics is read critically, it says as much: *Only if* there are no external effects, *only if* all markets are competitive, and *only when* all markets are in equilibrium is it true that a market economy will yield a Pareto optimal outcome. But despite these clear warnings, market enthusiasts insist that if left alone markets generally allocate resources very efficiently. This can only be true if: (1) disequilibrating forces are weak, (2) non-competitive market structures are uncommon, and (3) externalities are the exception, rather than the rule. There are good theoretical and empirical reasons to believe exactly the opposite in all three cases. A second line of defense holds that while free markets may be plagued by inefficiencies, it is possible to correct market failures through a variety of policies and thereby render them "reasonably" efficient. However, there are good practical reasons to believe it is unrealistic to expect such policies could ever render market systems even "reasonably" efficient.[6]

Equity: Not only do markets for natural, produced, and financial capital distribute income unfairly to their owners who expend no effort whatsoever, but also labor markets distribute income unfairly to people with different amounts of human capital. If the last hour of welding labor hired raises output and therefore revenue by more than the last hour of floor sweeping does, when employers compete with one another in labor markets for welders and sweepers they will bid

---

6 For my full argument regarding efficiency, interested readers should see "The Case Against Markets," *Journal of Economic Issues* 41, no. 4 (December 2007): 1,139–59.

the wage rate for welders up higher than the wage rate for sweepers—whether or not they are capitalist employers trying to maximize enterprise profits, or worker-owned enterprises trying to maximize profits per member.[7] This means that when labor is hired in labor markets, those who have more human capital, and therefore contribute more to enterprise output and revenues, will receive higher wages than those with less human capital. This is problematic because it means that a welder and sweeper who work equally hard in equally unpleasant circumstances will not be rewarded equally even though they make what we might call equal "sacrifices." In a market economy those with more human capital will receive more, even if they make no greater sacrifices, and those with less human capital will receive less, even if they sacrifice just as much or more.[8]

Moreover, there is no way to fix this problem in a market system without creating a great deal of inefficiency. If we intervene in the labor market and legislate wage rates we consider to be fair, but allow markets to determine how resources are allocated, not only will different kinds of labor be allocated inefficiently, but also the entire price structure of the economy will fail to reflect the opportunity costs of producing different goods and services leading to further inefficiencies. There is no getting around the dilemma: in a market economy we must either allow the market system to reward people unfairly, or, if we try to correct for inequities, we must tolerate even greater inefficiencies.[9]

Democracy: When all else fails—when they can no longer claim that markets lead to efficient or equitable outcomes—enthusiasts fall back

---

7 Worker-owned cooperatives may well have goals other than maximizing profits per member, but as long as this is *one* of their concerns the argument holds.

8 Most fail to understand how arbitrary differences in what economists call the "marginal revenue product" of different categories of labor truly are, and how little of those differences are due to how hard people work. Not only do differences in talent, education, and training come into play, differences in the quantity and quality of complimentary inputs, and differences in the scarcity of different categories of labor are all important in determining differences in marginal revenue products of labor. The important point is that unlike the amount of effort someone puts into his or her work, all these other influences on the value of output are largely beyond an individual's control.

9 For my full argument regarding equity see "Against the Market Economy: Advice to Venezuelan Friends," *Monthly Review* 59, no. 8 (January 2008).

on the claim that free markets promote economic and political democracy. But this defense of markets does not stand up under analysis any better than the others. Once we realize that economic freedom—the freedom to do as you wish with your person and property—is quite different from economic democracy—decision-making power in proportion to the degree one is affected—the case that markets promote economic democracy quickly unravels. Markets disenfranchise "third parties" affected by decisions a buyer and seller agree on. In a market "election" to decide what goods to produce, a wealthy person gets to vote thousands of times more than a poor person. Pretending that when market exchanges are voluntary there can be no coercion ignores the fact that a buyer or seller is often in a position to impose his will on the other who may have severely limited "outside" options. Finally, as every child knows, unequal economic power breeds unequal political power, so Milton Friedman's defense of markets, on grounds that the economic inequality markets generate is a virtue because any political cause can appeal for support from a wealthy benefactor, is patently absurd.[10]

Markets Never?

In a song in a famous Gilbert and Sullivan opera, the captain of the H.M.S. Pinafore insists that he never swears when talking to his crew. His crew responds, "What never?" to which the captain replies, "Not ever!" to which his crew asks again, "Not *ever*?" to which the captain finally replies "Well, *hardly* ever." Erik's position is to deny that markets should feature in an economic system even *hardly* ever is misguided and inflexible. In his words, because "there will necessarily be many trade-offs among competing values . . . markets, in one form or another, are likely to be a desirable part of solutions to some of the design problems." He argues that markets may be "a desirable part of solutions" to problems that a participatory economy would encounter. Given that a participatory economy is designed to eliminate the need for markets, if it can be shown that they are needed even here, it appears to follow that they are unavoidable in any system. The two situations he identifies as requiring markets are (1) during the implementation of the plan where coarse categories are refined and

10   For my full argument regarding democracy see "Why the Market Subverts Democracy," *American Behavioral Scientist* 52, no. 7 (March 2009): 1,006–22.

adjustments to unanticipated circumstances are made and (2) for the exchange of second-hand goods and tickets for entertainment events.

In round one I explained how refining coarse categories and making adjustments to a comprehensive plan could be done as the plan was being implemented. My purpose at the time was to refute the claim that practical problems of implementation were overwhelming and without solution, thereby rendering any kind of comprehensive planning impossible, or at least highly undesirable, by outlining several solutions, any of which would be adequate. In doing so I identified the important questions to consider when choosing among different possibilities: (1) to what extent producers or consumers will bear the burden of adjustments and (2) whether customers who change their demand for a good are treated any differently from customers who did not. I went on to point out that adjustments in supply and demand could be made with or without adjusting the planned "indicative" price used to credit producers and charge buyers, with different implications for who was bearing the burden of making adjustments. So, is it true that in a participatory economy we *never* have any markets?

The easy answer would be to take my cue from the captain of the Pinafore and sing, "Well, *hardly* ever." And if anyone wants to claim this means there may be a desirable role for markets in a participatory economy, so be it. However, as I pointed out when discussing the pros and cons of adjusting prices, in a participatory economy the purpose of making or not making adjustments in prices, and how much to adjust them, is to share the burdens of adjustments to the plan more equitably. I also explained three reasons why I do not believe in this case just because it may "look like a market and smell like a market," it truly is a market in any meaningful sense, which I need not repeat here because readers can revisit those arguments in my second contribution to the first round of our dialogue if need be.

As for the second situation, exchanging second-hand goods and tickets for entertainment events have nothing to do with what goods to produce, what events to schedule, or how many seats of different qualities there should be at events. So these exchanges have nothing to do with any decisions that planning addresses. However, Erik is correct that absent alternative solutions that are equally convenient people will want to trade used goods and tickets, as many do today over eBay. Again, the easy response would be "Well *hardly* ever," and concede that markets may have a role to play here as well. And when the time comes, if people want an eBay in a participatory economy, I am not so "inflexible" as to object.

However, even in this very limited context that has nothing to do with deciding what to produce, how to produce it, or how to distribute what has just been produced, I think it is worth considering non-market alternatives, or, at the very least, monitoring an eBay "solution" to prevent inequities and discourage antisocial behavior. A leading figure in Parecon Sweden is currently working on a proposal for how to credit people for returning used goods to distribution centers where redistribution can then be handled through normal participatory economic procedures. And a leading figure in the International Organization for a Participatory Society, (IOPS), in the UK is setting up an eBay for cooperatives to use that helps them express cooperative values concretely in exchanges among themselves and minimize inequities and dangers of antisocial behavior. I am happy there are others sufficiently concerned over whether or not convenient trading can foster antisocial behavior to be looking for alternatives even in situations like those Erik has raised.

The Socialist Case Against Markets

The dispassionate case against markets is clearly not enough. Erik was already aware of the dispassionate arguments that markets are inefficient, inequitable, and anti-democratic, which I and others have voiced, when he wrote:

> I do not see market transactions as such as intrinsically undesirable. What is undesirable are two things that are generally strongly linked to markets: first, the ways in which markets can enable people and organizations with specific kinds of power to gain advantages over others, and second, the way markets, *if inadequately regulated*, generate all sorts of destructive externalities and harms on people. But if those problems are minimized through various mechanisms, then the sheer fact of buyers and sellers of goods and services agreeing to exchange things at a mutually agreed-upon price is not, in and of itself, objectionable.

The problem with this attitude—which the dispassionate case against markets is powerless to affect—is that it is insufficiently fearful.

This attitude mistakenly assumes that only the bad outcomes are problematic—the inefficiencies, inequities, and violations of democracy—which therefore should be addressed through appropriate means. However, beyond the bad outcomes there is a more fundamental problem. I tried to flag this problem in the first round of our dialogue by expressing my concern in a very simple way:

> When a division of labor is coordinated by markets those who take advantage of others are often rewarded while those who behave in socially responsible ways are often punished for having done so. For this reason markets act like a cancer that undermines efforts to build and deepen participatory, equitable cooperation.

Why?

In every market transaction, the seller is trying to take advantage of the buyer, and the buyer is trying to take advantage of the seller. If we play "word association" and say "market," economists are likely to respond with "mutual benefit," whereas normal people would be more likely to respond with "haggle." The problem is not that one response is right and one is wrong. The problem is that *both* responses are correct! Moreover, in every market transaction both the buyer and seller have every incentive to ignore the interests of anyone else who might be affected by their decision. This is not only undemocratic and inefficient, it is a second way in which market relations not only fail to provide means for people to take the interests of others into account, they systematically punish any who attempt to practice solidarity. In other words, markets "work" by stimulating greed and fear while undermining trust and solidarity needed to build the economics of equitable cooperation. In short, markets are cancer to the socialist project.

I use the word "cancer" not to evoke powerful negative emotions, but because cancer begins as a small malignancy, a cellular dysfunction, which spreads until it destroys an entire organism. And that is the image I wished to convey for why we should fear permitting markets to continue to play a role in a truly desirable economy. That is why we should search for other ways to respond to situations that make markets tempting. As Erik pointed out, people *will* spontaneously engage in market behavior, and using markets for particular purposes even in an economy, where what to produce and how to produce it is first determined by a comprehensive production plan, *will* often appear convenient. So it is easy to understand why people may feel that objecting to even "a dash" of markets is overly zealous and inflexible. Which would indeed be true if a dash of markets were like a dash of salt. But if instead a dash of markets is like a dash of cancer that can spread to undermine the socialist project, that is quite another matter altogether.

In a sense this is a debate over what is a realistic attitude regarding markets. Is there good reason to fear them? The dispassionate case against markets refutes every positive claim made on behalf of markets except that people often find them convenient, which I do not deny. But when presented in this way the case against markets fails to convey what I believe is a fully warranted sense of danger. And acknowledging that there are policies available to mitigate damages, which I also do not deny, leaves the impression that in a world that is inevitably imperfect some markets can hardly be problematic. This is the attitude of someone who argues that markets are not intrinsically bad, it is only the negative consequences of markets, not markets themselves that are problematic. Nobody would say that about cancer. This is the attitude of someone who points out that we can correct for inequities, externalities, and market disequilibria, even if only imperfectly. Nobody would agree to introduce a little cancer if it were convenient, because chemotherapy treatments are available. This is the attitude of someone who reasons there must surely be a role for markets as well as planning in the "optimal" economy because planning has its weaknesses as well as strengths, just as markets do. Nobody would say that an optimal life includes exposure to cancer.

While this is not the place to go into particulars, I believe there is overwhelming historical evidence to back my fears. Despite strong measures favoring worker self-management and retention of public ownership, because the Basic Law of Worker Self-Management also replaced planning with markets in 1951, it gave rise to increasingly antisocial behavior and rising inequality in Yugoslavia. Market reforms that retained public ownership but did not grant workers self-management in the Soviet Union, Eastern Europe, China, and Vietnam invariably generated similar antisocial behavior and rising inequality. And the dilemma worker-owned cooperatives face as they try to reconcile commercial and cooperative goals when subjected to market competition are well documented.

Real Utopias and Transformation

While Erik and I use different language, our thinking about what he calls "social transformation" and I call "transition strategy" is very similar. Erik talks of "ruptural" vs. "symbiotic" strategies. I talk of "system change" vs. "reform" and how radicals and reformers better learn to work more productively with each other. Erik talks of "interstitial" strategies. I talk of creating "imperfect experiments in equitable cooperation," or "prefigurative" organizing. But we are talking about the same things, making the same distinctions, and for the most part we come to the same conclusions. Since I concur with Erik's summary evaluation of the historical record regarding weaknesses in each strategy, I will concentrate on digging deeper into *why* each has failed historically.

Regarding ruptural strategies, Erik writes:

> Ruptural strategies have a grandiose, romantic appeal to critics of capitalism, but the historical record is pretty dismal. There are no cases in which socialism as defined here—a deeply democratic and egalitarian organization of power relations within an economy—has been a robust result of a ruptural strategy of transformation of capitalism. Ruptural strategies seem in practice more prone to result in authoritarian statism than democratic socialism.

True, but the important question is why? Many conclude that "ruptural" or wholesale system change is incompatible with changes that are "deeply democratic and egalitarian." I think the problem lies elsewhere if a build-up to "ruptural" system change does not involve enough people fighting for reforms and lacks enough experiments creating institutions that "prefigure" deeply democratic and egalitarian behavior. Overall, therefore, I am more positive about the prospects of ruptural strategies when movements committed to democratic societies prepare for them properly—which is fortunate because I also believe they are more likely to play a necessary role in achieving desirable "system change" as explained below.

As for interstitial strategies, Erik writes that they "may produce improvements in the lives of people and pockets of more democratic-egalitarian practices, but they also have nowhere succeeded in significantly eroding capitalist power relations." True, but again the important question is why? I think it is because concentrating exclusively on building prefigurative institutions has two predictable pitfalls: First and foremost, exclusive focus on building alternatives to capitalism is too isolating. Until the non-capitalist sector is large, the livelihoods of most people will depend on winning reforms in the capitalist sector, and therefore that is where most people will become engaged. But concentrating exclusively on experiments in equitable cooperation will also not work because the rules of capitalism put alternative institutions at a disadvantage compared to capitalist firms they must compete against, and because market forces drive non-capitalist institutions to abandon cooperative principles. Unlike liberated territories in third-world countries fighting to overthrow imperialism last century, in the advanced economies we will have to build our experiments in equitable cooperation inside our capitalist economies. So our experiments will always be fully exposed to competitive pressures and the culture of capitalism. Maintaining cooperative principles in alternative experiments under these conditions requires high levels of political commitment, which it is reasonable to expect from activists committed to building "a new world," but unreasonable to expect from everyone.

Erik writes about the failures of reform organizing at greater length:

As for symbiotic strategies, in the most successful instances of social democracy they have certainly resulted in a more humane capitalism, with less poverty, less inequality, and less insecurity, but they have done so in ways which stabilize capitalism and leave intact the core powers of capital. Any advance of symbiotic strategies historically that appeared to potentially threaten those core powers was massively resisted by capital. The reaction of Swedish capitalists to proposals for serious union involvement in control over investment in the late 1970s is one of the best-known examples. These are all reasonable objections.

In my own critique of Swedish social democracy[11] I also finger the failure to push through with the Meidner plan and wage-earner fund

---

11   See Hahnel, "Social Democracy: Losing the Faith," Chapter 5 in *Economic Justice and Democracy: From Competition to Cooperation* (Oxon and New York: Routledge, 2005).

in the mid-1970s, when progressive forces arguably had Swedish capitalists "on the run," as a critical mistake. Progressives should have disarmed Swedish capitalists by taking away their power over jobs and investment. Whether Swedish social democrats could have won a political "stare down" with Swedish capitalists in 1975 we will never know because they never tried. But with hindsight we do know that the rollback of social democratic reforms that took decades to win began soon afterwards, and neoliberalism in Sweden has become ever more ascendant. More generally, I point to what Michael Harrington called the "grand social democratic compromise," which he defined as "settling for a situation in which social democrats would regulate and tax capitalism but not challenge it in any fundamental way." However, I believe not even Harrington appreciated the full consequences of the compromise. It is one thing to say: We are committed to democracy above all else. Therefore we promise that as long as a majority of the population does not want to replace capitalism, we have no intentions of trying to do so. It is quite another thing to say: Despite our best efforts we have failed to convince a majority of the population that capitalism is fundamentally incompatible with economic justice and democracy and environmental sustainability. Therefore we will cease to challenge the legitimacy of the capitalist system and confine our efforts to reforming it. The first position is one I believe the movement for equitable cooperation must abide by in the future, while the second is one we must learn from history to reject.

In any case, reforms alone cannot achieve equitable cooperation because as long as the institutions of private enterprise and markets are left in place to reinforce antisocial behavior based on greed and fear, progress toward equitable cooperation will be limited, and the danger of retrogression will be ever present. Moreover, reform campaigns undermine their leaders' commitment to full economic justice and democracy in a number of ways, and do little to demonstrate that equitable cooperation is possible, or establish new norms and expectations.

However, most importantly I agree with Erik's conclusion about what the best strategy seems to be for the moment, at least in the United States: "I think the best prospect for the future in developed capitalist countries is a strategic orientation mainly organized around the interplay of interstitial and symbiotic strategies, with perhaps periodic episodes involving elements of ruptural strategy." I have argued at length elsewhere that in the United States: (1) Desirable system change—a "ruptural transformation"—will not come until we have strengthened our forces through much more successful reform and prefigurative organizing. (2) Reform and prefigurative organizing each play a critical role the other cannot. And (3) each of these kinds of organizing help counter the predictable pitfalls of the other when pursued alone.[12]

Erik also sees symbiotic and interstitial organizing complementing each other:

> Through interstitial strategies, activists and communities can build and strengthen real utopian economic institutions embodying democratic-egalitarian principles, where this is possible. Symbiotic strategies through the state can help open up greater space and support for these interstitial innovations. The interplay between interstitial and symbiotic strategies could then create a trajectory of deepening socialist elements within the hybrid capitalist economic ecosystem.

I agree—reform campaigns counteract the tendency for prefigurative projects to be self-isolating, while expanding experiments in equitable cooperation helps activists fighting for system change "keep the faith," demonstrates concretely to skeptics that equitable cooperation works, and allows us to discover how we can cooperate with one another more effectively through experimentation.

Erik and I both understand that elites can force confrontation. He writes: "While elites may become resigned to a diminution of power, they are unlikely to gracefully embrace the prospects. While symbiotic transformations help solve problems within capitalism, they often are not optimal for elites and are thus resisted. This means that a key element of ruptural strategies—confrontations between opposing organized social forces in which there are winners and losers—will be a part of any plausible trajectory of sustainable social empowerment." As I have already said, we should not be surprised if

---

12　For a more extensive presentation of my suggestions regarding transition strategy, see the last four chapters in *Economic Justice and Democracy: From Competition to Cooperation.*

elites refuse to abide by majority opinion when reform and prefigurative organizing threatens their privileges and power, and we should not hesitate to disarm them precisely in order to be able to continue with programs that have majority support. However, I am disappointed with Erik's formulation of how we should behave when such situations arise: "The purpose of such confrontations, however, is not a systemic rupture with capitalist dominance, but rather creating more space for the interplay of interstitial and symbiotic strategies." At some point "creating more space for interplay" must give way to "a systemic rupture with capitalist dominance," which means abolishing the institutional basis for their dominance, the private enterprise market system. When decisive moments come one either defeats an enemy and disarms him to prevent war from erupting anew, or one fails to do so. In moments of confrontation unfortunately, in my opinion, those with a personal inclination toward symbiotic and interstitial strategies are all too likely to make the same mistake Swedish social democrats made in 1975. At moments when those who hesitate are lost, leadership with more "ruptural inclinations" becomes more socially useful. Why, when we get the chance, should we hesitate to drive our stake through the vampire's heart?

Conclusion
Erik writes in his conclusion:

> Instead of a unitary institutional design . . . the configurations of social empowerment open up space for a wide diversity of institutional forms . . . These diverse forms all increase social power, but they do not point to an integrated, comprehensive system driven by a single institutional design principle of the sort proposed by Robin in his analysis of participatory economics.

I hope it is clear by now that I not only regard "institutional pluralism *in transition*," including markets, as a practical necessity, but also appreciate that pluralism in transition provides a valuable way to test different ideas about how best to organize economic activities. However, in my opinion "institutional pluralism of the destination" can be an excuse for imprecise reasoning that fails to follow assumptions through to their logical conclusions.

In today's world an alternative economic "vision" needs to accomplish three goals: (1) It must open people's eyes to the possibility of a much more desirable way of organizing our economic activities. In other words, it must be inspiring. (2) It must answer reasonable doubts about whether or not the "vision" is a real possibility rather than merely a fantasy arising from bitter disappointment—much like the concept of heaven. To do this it must demonstrate concretely how questions that must be answered in any economy could be answered, and how problems that will inevitably arise could be addressed. In other words, it must convince people the vision is feasible for humans who are *both* self- and other-regarding. (3) It must challenge popular misconceptions about what is consistent or inconsistent with our goals. In other words, it must help clarify what the pursuit of economic justice and democracy as well as environmental sustainability require.

While Erik no longer misinterprets the model of a participatory economy as a strategic transitional program, I think he still underestimates the usefulness of elaborating rigorous models of future economic systems. I conclude my contribution to our dialogue by reminiscing about reactions the model of a participatory economy has provoked over the past two decades, which indirectly testifies to the value and limits of this kind of intellectual exercise.

Over the past twenty years I have sometimes had to respond to criticisms I anticipated. I expected people to challenge our proposal to base any differences in income on differences in workers' efforts as judged by co-workers. And I expected people to question the desirability of balancing jobs for empowerment. And over the past two decades many have questioned the wisdom of asking worker councils to reward effort and balance jobs for empowerment—although Erik does not. However, since it was widely believed that in a modern economy with an elaborate division of labor there simply is no alternative to a market system or authoritarian comprehensive planning, I expected people to challenge our claim to have found a highly democratic way to arrive at an efficient comprehensive economic plan. However, few have challenged our claim that the participatory planning procedure belies the claim that there is no alternative to markets and authoritarian planning. And frankly, this has surprised me.

I initially thought the major stumbling block was that many who were disenchanted with the market system no longer believed there was any feasible way to engage in comprehensive economic planning that was not authoritarian and/or inefficient. So I expected critics to challenge our claim to have solved that problem. However, for the most part critics have not argued that our procedure will fail to produce a feasible plan. They have not argued that the plan arrived at would be inefficient, or that it would fail to adequately protect the environment. Except for a few anarchists who insist that the IFB—which in fact has no discretionary power whatsoever—is nonetheless an authoritarian central planning bureau in disguise, critics have not disputed that our procedure is thoroughly democratic, or that it affords worker and consumer councils more autonomy than most dreamed democratic planning ever could.

It is true that some have criticized participatory planning as a nightmare of endless meetings where a "dictatorship of the sociable" would inevitably end up settling on an inefficient plan. But those who make these arguments have either failed to read our actual proposal, or utterly failed to comprehend it. Those who voice this criticism confuse our procedure with a common conception of democratic planning that is completely different. We most emphatically do *not* propose that worker and consumer councils send delegates lacking estimates of opportunity and social costs of making things to meetings that would be endless, to come up with a comprehensive plan which would be inefficient. In fact, we agree with critics that any attempt to go about comprehensive economic planning in this way would prove disastrous, and what we have proposed is an *alternative* to this naïve and misguided notion of how to organize comprehensive planning democratically. In sum, these critics do not engage our actual proposal for how to arrive at a comprehensive plan, but instead criticise a completely different idea we explicitly reject.

But most criticisms of our planning proposal have nothing to do with how we propose to arrive at a comprehensive plan. Whether consciously or not, most critics have challenged the desirability of *any* comprehensive economic plan, independent of how it is generated, or whatever desirable properties it may have. Most criticisms are about problems that arise when we move onto implementing a plan. Critics ask how broad categories in a comprehensive plan, like shoes, would be turned into detailed items, like size 6½, purple women's high-heeled, leatherless shoes with a yellow toe. Some, like Seth Ackerman writing in *Jacobin* magazine, assume there is no answer to this question and dismiss all comprehensive planning as impossible. Others, like Erik, recognize that this problem is not insurmountable, but argue that we will find markets helpful when solving it. Critics ask what will happen when unforeseen circumstances arise and the plan needs to be adjusted. Again, some argue that market systems adjust far better than planned economies to unforeseen events, and therefore should be preferred for this reason alone. Others, like Erik, argue that markets can help us make necessary adjustments in the plan, and also handle exchanges of second-hand goods. But none of this has anything to do with how to come up with a comprehensive economic plan in the first place—which was the problem we tackled initially.

A part of me feels like I have won the war I volunteered to fight, and would now like to retire—with full honors of course. Surely there must be other volunteers willing to answer questions about how best to address practical problems that arise when we start to implement any comprehensive economic plan. If we have demonstrated there is a way to arrive at a comprehensive plan for the economy that is not authoritarian but instead fully democratic; if we have demonstrated the plan arrived at will use resources efficiently; if we have shown that the procedure generates credible estimates of the damage from pollution and charges polluters accordingly; if we have shown that the procedure generates credible estimates of social benefits and costs, allowing worker and consumer councils to self-police with little fanfare; if we have shown how all this can be done without sending delegates to the kind of planning meetings that would be unproductive nightmares . . . isn't this enough? If not, who moved the finish line?

Looking back on questions critics have raised about our planning proposal over the past twenty years, it is now apparent to me that there were always two questions, not one: (1) Is it possible to arrive at a desirable comprehensive national plan in a desirable way? (2) Is it desirable to use comprehensive plans to run our economies? The first is the question we set out to answer many years ago. But if the answer to the second question is "no," it makes no difference what the answer to the first question is. There is no reason to search for a desirable process to generate a desirable comprehensive plan if we don't want to use a comprehensive plan in any case. On the other hand, if the answer to the first question is "no," there is no need to consider the second question if we have already rejected authoritarian planning.

I believe the participatory planning procedure has now stood the test of time as a satisfactory answer to the first question. Yes, we can generate an attractive comprehensive plan through a process that is quite appealing. Which is why I think criticisms of participatory planning are now either criticisms of a planning procedure that is not ours, or criticisms of comprehensive planning in any form. That is, criticisms that would apply equally to any and all comprehensive plans, irrespective of how they were generated or how desirable their properties. As long as people believed the answer to the first question was "no," they did not have to think about the second question. On the other hand, people would not be raising questions about implementing comprehensive plans if they did not now accept the possibility of generating a desirable comprehensive plan through a process that is also desirable.

So while I anticipated having to defend the virtues of the participatory planning procedure over alternative ways of arriving at a comprehensive plan, instead I have more often had to defend comprehensive planning in general as an alternative to a market system. In this dialogue and elsewhere, I have tried to respond to questions people raise about how comprehensive plans can be implemented and adjusted. In truth I find this an odd exercise since a number of large national economies implemented comprehensive economic plans successfully for many decades during the twentieth century. But memories are short, confusion over what went wrong and what did not in the centrally planned economies runs rampant, and most who ask such questions never lived in anything other than a market economy themselves and therefore understandably have little sense of how a non-market system works. But I should be clear: I treat these problems as practical problems for which we must only find *adequate* answers. Because, provided there are adequate answers, we need not abandon comprehensive planning—which we have good reasons to prefer provided it can be done democratically and efficiently—in favor of a market system—which we have good reasons for rejecting.

In other words, for me solutions to problems of implementation and adjustment need not be perfect, but only adequate. And when there are multiple ways to implement and adjust plans, I believe not only convenience but also the possibility of generating antisocial behavior should be carefully considered.

CHAPTER 6

Final Thoughts

Erik Olin Wright

In my final contribution to this dialogue on alternatives to capitalism I will focus on a number of specific ways in which Robin's approach to these matters differs from my own. It should certainly be clear to everyone that our dialogue is not antagonistic. There are, to be sure, some real differences in our judgments, but these are disagreements within a common project of trying to grapple with the problem of thinking beyond capitalism. The convergence of our views is much more fundamental than these points of disagreement. In particular we share a common critique of capitalism, a common understanding of the central values we would like to see realised in a post-capitalist society, and a common commitment to progressive reform within capitalism as a necessary part of the (possible) transformation beyond capitalism. Within this context of such shared understandings, what I hope to do here is not mainly defend my positions against Robin's last piece, but rather revisit a variety of themes we have been discussing throughout this dialogue to give as much precision as I can to the nature of our remaining disagreements.

1. What Is Wrong with Markets?

In Robin's comment on my approach to socialism and real utopias he correctly identifies our disagreement over the moral implications of markets. Both of us agree that *unfettered* markets systematically generate negative consequences—especially negative externalities, intensifications of inequalities, and concentrations of power. And we both argue that these consequences can be mitigated by appropriate countermeasures (although perhaps I am more optimistic than Robin about the extent to which the potential harms of markets can be prevented with appropriate public policies). We also both believe that whatever problems there are with markets as such are intensified in capitalism. Where we differ is in our assessment of whether in addition to these *side-effects* of markets, markets are *intrinsically harmful* to central values of a democratic-egalitarian society, especially the value of solidarity. Here is how Robin formulates this issue:

> In every market transaction, the seller is trying to take advantage of the buyer, and the buyer is trying to take advantage of the seller . . . In other words, markets "work" by stimulating greed and fear while undermining trust and solidarity needed to build the economics of equitable cooperation. In short, markets are cancer to the socialist project.
>
> [. . .]
>
> As Erik pointed out, people will spontaneously engage in market behavior, and using markets for particular purposes even in an economy where what to produce and how to produce it is first determined by a comprehensive production plan, will often appear convenient. So it is easy to understand why people may feel that objecting to even "a dash" of markets is overly zealous and inflexible. Which would indeed be true if a dash of markets were like a dash of salt. But if instead a dash of markets is like a dash of cancer that can spread to undermine the socialist project, that is quite another matter altogether.
>
> [. . .]
>
> The dispassionate case against markets refutes every positive claim made for markets, except that people often find them convenient, which I do not deny . . . Nobody would say that an optimal life includes a proper dose of cancer.

The metaphor of cancer, of course, is a powerfully evocative way of characterizing markets as having intrinsic harms, but is this really apt?[1] Is it true that fear and greed are inherently the motivational

---

1 Robin's co-author in the development of the participatory economics model, Michael Albert, uses an even more provocative metaphor to describe the presence of markets in an otherwise participatory economy. He sees markets like slavery: "Having a little market in a parecon is a bit like having a little slavery in a democracy, though even less tenable. The logic of markets invalidates the logic of participatory planning and of the whole parecon, and it is also imperial, once it exists trying to spread as far and wide as it can." (Michael Albert, *Parecon* [London and New York: Verso, 2003], 79).

states of actors engaged in voluntary, uncoordinated, decentralized agreements to produce and sell things to each other? Is it true that engaging in market practices between consenting adults necessarily embodies and fosters antisocial values?

Before directly engaging this question, I would like to make a side point on the metaphor of markets-as-cancer. An alternative metaphor would be markets-as-carcinogenic-agents rather than as cancer itself. In this alternative metaphor, the presence of markets poses some risks, one of which is the fostering of antisocial norms and behavior. But it is no longer the case that one can unequivocally say that no one would choose a "dash of risk," even in the case of a risk for cancer. Indeed, in Robin's own analysis of participatory planning he argues that under conditions of strong equality and democratic empowerment, people in a community ought to be able to opt for whatever level of pollution they want so long as they are properly compensated for this by the polluters. This is a critical—and I would add valuable—aspect of the iterative planning process between producers and people in the broader society affected by the externalities of the production process, since it forces producers to take into account the full social costs of their production.[2] I endorse that aspect of Robin's model as part of his deep effort to realize the democratic value that people ought to participate in decisions to the extent that they are affected by the consequences of those decisions. The implication of this commitment to democratic values, however, is that there is nothing strange about voluntarily choosing a certain level of risk for cancer (since pollution often brings such risks) given the trade-offs people face between such risks and other things they care about. If allowing markets is like this—they pose risks—then it would be reasonable for people to make choices about this as well.

---

2 This aspect of Robin's model goes against the views of many radical environmentalists who broadly argue for minimizing pollution rather than leaving this up to the preferences of people who will have to live with the pollution. Robin correctly recognizes that there are real trade-offs people face in opting for no risk, and while it may be difficult to finely calibrate how to navigate those trade-offs, so long as people have good information and are on equal footing in balancing their priorities, then people should be able to choose the balance between income and the level of pollution. This is what is accomplished through the iterated planning process on negative externalities.

But is this the right way to think about the impact of markets on motivations and values? Or are markets, as Robin argues, actually like cancer itself, which suggests that inevitably the presence of markets will foster corrosive antisocial values? I disagree with this diagnosis of the intrinsic effects of uncoordinated voluntary exchange. Rather, I see the extent to which market relations embody motivations of fear and greed is highly variable and depends on the specific cultural forms and social relations within which those market processes are embedded. This is a standard argument in the sociological analysis of markets. Emile Durkheim refers to this as the "noncontractual elements of contract" and Karl Polanyi as the social embeddedness of markets. The basic idea is that markets are always existing in an environment of internalized norms and informal social regulation (as well as, of course, formal legal regulation), and this deeply shapes the experience of people within market exchanges and the kinds of dispositions they bring into those relations. In some market environments there are high levels of trust and reciprocity, without the pervasive fear and anxiety associated with brutally competitive markets. In other markets the aphorism "buyer beware" properly describes the exchange relation.

This Durkheimian sociological understanding of the normative dimension of markets is quite alien to the way markets are typically understood by economists. For most economists, market agents are purely selfish, rational, calculative actors. This is what sociologists traditionally characterize as an "under-socialized" view of people.[3] In a world of people who are disconnected from reciprocity-based social relations and normative commitments, then it is reasonable to see markets as intrinsically reinforcing and spreading antisocial motivations and practices. But I see no reason to imagine that in an economy dominated by participatory, democratic, egalitarian relations and values, the co-presence of market relations within certain aspects of

---

3   Mark Granovetter, in "Economic Action and Social Structure: The Problem of Embeddedness," (*American Journal of Sociology*, no. 91 [November 3, 1985]: 481–510) famously contrasts the characteristic "undersocialized view of man" in economics with an "oversocialized view of man" in much sociology. While the former sees people as atomistic, self-directed, rational actors, the latter sees people as following scripts imposed on them by culture. Granovetter offers an intermediary view of socially-embedded economic action.

economic practices would have these properties. These motivational states are not intrinsic to market processes as such; they are only intrinsic to the atomistic, normatively unconstrained markets of economics models. In a capitalist economy—especially a neo-liberal capitalist economy in which markets are indeed relatively disconnected from community reciprocities, competition is destructive, and the cultural formation of people encourages manipulative selfish strategies—markets do indeed embody and foster greed and fear, but this is not because of something intrinsic to the sheer fact of market processes but to the social form of those markets in capitalism.[4]

Let me give an imperfect parallel example to illustrate my point here: competition within sports. Some radical egalitarians have argued that competition within sports and games intrinsically fosters status hierarchies and various types of anti-solidaristic sentiments. Players in a sport want to win and this means "defeating" an "opponent." Winners are better than losers. Aggressiveness is valued. And so forth. Other people contend that competition in sports can be governed by norms of good sportsmanship, of fair play and camaraderie, and that whatever status inequalities are generated by sports could be contained in ways that would make them relatively benign. In particular, if other kinds of rewards—in particular wealth and power—are not connected to being successful in sports, then normatively regulated competitive sports need not be corrosive of egalitarian social solidarity.

I do not think the question of the moral status and cultural effects of competition in sports is a settled issue. It is possible that, in the

---

4 To fully sort out the contrast between my views and Robin's on this issue would require a discussion of some quite difficult methodological issues about the relation between abstract concepts and their concrete realization. When Robin claims that fear and greed are *intrinsic* to markets rather than a variable *effect* of markets in specific contexts (as is the case for negative externalities), he is relying on a particular way of thinking about the abstract "pure" concept of "markets" in which the fundamental nature of markets can be analyzed independently of the concrete institutional and cultural forms in which they may occur, and at that level of abstraction fear and greed are inherent features. He then assumes that because these are inherent features at the most abstract level of analysis they remain inherent features at the concrete institutional, cultural, and social forms which markets take in the world. My position, in contrast, is that these concrete cultural and social forms are internalized within markets and can alter the consequences of what might otherwise be seen as their inherent properties.

end, competitive sports are always pernicious, that they intrinsically foster socially harmful forms of status inequality regardless of the broader social context. Anti-competition activists in the 1970s created a range of "new games" rooted in cooperative values and some of these in fact were reasonably enjoyable, at least to some people.[5] Perhaps in a post-capitalist world with a participatory economy, people will abandon competitive sports just as Robin hopes that they will completely abandon markets. But it is also possible that in the context of the cultural forms that are consolidated within such a world, whatever the negative effects of competition in sports will be minimal, and competitive sports will flourish as a human activity because many people will find them interesting and fun to play.

2. But Is There Anything Actually *Desirable* about Markets?

Even if one accepts my argument that markets, understood as unco-ordinated decentralized voluntary exchanges, do not *intrinsically* generate antisocial behavior, nevertheless I acknowledge that they may have a *tendency* to do so. Why not try to completely eliminate all social practices that have the potential of generating such harms? The only reason to allow a space for market processes is that they promote some other positive value that we care about and a complete elimina-tion of all market processes would harm those values. There are two positive values a constrained use of markets might advance: "conven-ience" and risk-taking initiatives.

Convenience

Robin acknowledges that even in a broadly democratic participatory economy people might opt to use markets in some contexts, but if they do so it will be because of "convenience," with the implication that this is to be contrasted with a deeper dedication to democratic partici-patory principles. As quoted above: "People *will* spontaneously engage in market behavior, and using markets for particular purposes even in an economy where what to produce and how to produce it is first determined by a comprehensive production plan, *will* often appear convenient." The use of the word "convenient" here suggests that this reflects a kind of weakness of will or moral laziness. Certainly,

---

5   For a description of new games, see inewgames.com.

if markets really are like cancer, people would be making a mistake in deciding that a "dash of markets" is convenient. But if the greed-and-fear-inducing property of markets depends upon how they are embedded in other social institutions and the ways in which they embody specific pro-social norms, then in a broadly democratic-egalitarian economic system "convenience" could actually reflect positive values for which it is reasonable that people would think about balance and trade-offs.

"Convenience" is a way of talking about the time and effort for doing one thing rather than another. Time and effort are valuable, and thus it may be reasonable to trade convenience off against other values, depending on the situation. It is even reasonable to give up some degree of taking into account total social costs of production (the negative externality problem) or other aspects of resource-use efficiency for a significant increase in convenience. Robin is quite confident that a pure participatory economy in which all aspects of economic activity were processed through the participatory planning mechanisms would not take up a lot of time and effort. He therefore believes that there would not be much convenience gained from allowing any market-like processes into the system. (And, as already noted, he also believes there would always be significant costs, since markets are like cancer and this would be corrosive of the participatory process itself). I lack Robin's confidence that participatory mechanisms will work as smoothly as he believes and that the time and effort involved will be minimal. My expectation, therefore, is that "convenience" will matter to people for good reasons and this will provide legitimate grounds for people to choose a dose of markets (probably more than just a dash).

The trade-off between convenience and fully banishing market processes is, I believe, a significant issue in the iterative planning process for consumers. Robin admits that many—perhaps most people—will not spend much time on planning their consumption for the next year. They will only provide very rough indicators of what they plan to consume, largely based on what they did the previous year, and certainly nothing like a fine-grained account of specific, detailed products. Why? Because they don't want to spend the time and energy to do so. They opt for convenience. I agree with Robin that this is perfectly fine. But the result is that the post-planning adjustments to initial allocations are likely to be quite large and—more importantly—may function very much like market adjustments that shape both prices and quantities of things produced. To avoid such market-like adjustments would require people to spend a great deal more time in carefully planning their future consumption, which would be an unacceptable sacrifice of "convenience." I will discuss this trade-off in more detail in the section on hybrids below.

Risk-taking initiative

As I explained in my initial comment on Robin's model, another aspect of economic life in which I can imagine people democratically embracing a space for market processes would be to allow certain forms of entrepreneurial risk-taking. In any participatory process of investment planning there will inevitably be a range of investment projects that get rejected, which is fine. But it is easy to imagine that under these conditions there will be people with rejected proposals who are nevertheless able to mobilize capital from personal networks or personal savings—after all, an effort-based income system can allow very hard-working people, especially if they are part of a group, to amass over a period of time considerable savings. The question then is whether there will be a strict prohibition on people launching a project using these "private" resources without getting prior permission from the relevant planning council. My prediction is that in a broadly participatory economy some space will be allowed for more chaotic investment processes because this will be seen as an all-things-considered better mix of planning and uncoordinated spontaneity than a system requiring that every economic project get permission go through the standard planning process.

The importance of trade-offs

The presence of some space for democratically constrained markets within a participatory economy may thus be the optimal mix given trade-offs of various values. Acknowledging such trade-offs in the ideal social "destination" of a process of social transformation, however, does not imply watering down the ideal; it just says that the ideal economic system must try to realize a plurality of values and that the different values themselves are sometimes in tension. This is not about the practical necessity tolerating imperfections in the ideal during a transition; it is about the optimal institutional configuration in the destination to realize a complex set of partially conflicting values.

To help clarify my fundamental point here, let me discuss another case that also bears on core values involved in a participatory economy: the difficult problem of implementing in an optimal way the democratic value. Both Robin and I endorse the radical democratic value that people should participate in decisions to the extent that they are affected by them. If a decision only affects oneself, then that decision can be autonomously made without anyone else's involvement; but if a decision affects other people, then they should be co-participants in the decision *to the extent that they are affected*. Now, this is the correct principle. The question then is how precisely we should understand the practical trade-offs in its implementation. In reality, nearly everything we do has effects on other people, so it is impossible to actually involve everyone affected by a decision in a proportionate role in the decision. The result is that some kind of line of demarcation has to be drawn between the public and the private domains of decision-making: inside the private domain, however that is defined, one need not get permission from anyone else to make choices. This boundary is, of course, not pre-social, not some "natural" line of demarcation. It is socially constructed, and in a democratic society, constructed through democratic deliberation. But once created it defines the limits of collaborative, democratic decision-making.

One way of looking at this demarcation of the public/private boundary is that it is simply a practical concession to the complexity of life. Another way of looking at the issue is that even if magically one could involve everyone in every decision that had any effect on them we would not want to do this. Individual self-directed autonomy is also a value, and a full implementation of the democratic proportionality principle would involve too severe a restriction on autonomy. This is a tricky issue, of course, and it opens a space for a lot of contestation about how much autonomous self-direction is desirable. Billboards impinge on other people. Some messages may be offensive. Some may be offensive to a small group of people and not others. Should everyone who is negatively affected by a billboard have a proportionate say in allowing it? Or do we value autonomy of individual expression and want to allow a fairly broad scope for people erecting billboards to express their views? These are difficult issues that cannot be resolved by simply invoking a no-trade-off rule for democratic values.

As long as we are trying to realize multiple values and ideals, then worrying about these kinds of trade-offs is inherent in the design of any social institution. In the case of economic institutions, democracy, solidarity, and equality are critical values, but so are convenience and autonomous individual initiative. The optimal trade-off across these values is likely to require a space for some market-processes within a participatory economy.

3. The Hidden Infusion of Marketish Processes Within a Participatory Economy: the Problem of Hybrids

I make the argument that even if we had a participatory economy fully in place, we cannot know now what the real weight of the adjustment processes within the implementation of plans will look like. Robin acknowledges that there will be lots of adjustments to plans. But he also assumes that these adjustments will be relatively small compared to planned allocations, and thus that the system as a whole is really a planned system of allocations with minor adjustments, rather than a planned system which imposes constraints on lively market-like processes. I do not think we can confidently know now whether, in such a possible world, post-planning adjustments will be small relative to initial expectations or large, and whether or not the adjustment process will look a lot like markets or something else. Robin writes:

> I also explained three reasons why I do not believe in this case [i.e. post-planning adjustments] just because it may "look like a market and smell like a market," it truly is a market in any meaningful sense.

This is a key issue—looking and smelling like a market but not "truly" being a market. This is part of what I mean by saying that all real economic systems are hybrids of different principles. Of course, market-like adjustments within a participatory planning world is not the same as a "market system" or a "free market," but these market processes could still play a critical role in coordinating actual production through feedback processes based on supply and demand, lowering prices, and increasing and shifting production in response to what people actually do rather than what they anticipate doing.

The key to my diagnosis of the actual infusion of market processes within even Robin's model of a participatory economy is the claim that the adjustments, especially if large, are really a variety of a hybrid market process. Robin clearly does not think this is the right way to think about this. In the conclusion of his commentary on my essay he discusses the mistakes people have made in criticizing the processes of comprehensive participatory planning:

> Critics ask how broad categories in a comprehensive plan, like shoes, would be turned into detailed items, like size 6½, purple women's high-heeled, leatherless shoes with a yellow toe. Some, like Seth Ackerman writing in *Jacobin* magazine, assume there is no answer to this question and dismiss all comprehensive planning as impossible. Others, like Erik, recognize that this problem is not insurmountable, but argue that we will find markets helpful when solving it.

He rejects my argument and instead describes the process by which actual production hones in on the right number of "size 6½, purple women's high-heeled, leatherless shoes with a yellow toe" as non-market adjustments. My position is certainly not that the solution requires introducing a full-blown, autonomous "market system" into the economy, but rather that the introduction of effective adjustment processes is likely to have strong market-like features—they would look like a market and smell like a market—in that they would involve "buyers and sellers of goods and services agreeing to exchange things at mutually agreed upon prices." The actual exchanges that result from this process (in contrast to the anticipated plans), in turn, would be data that would feedback into ongoing decisions about how much of different things to produce. This is a real feedback process, which is embedded in the post-planning uncoordinated interactions of buyers and sellers and the adjustments that emerge out of those interactions. These significant market-like adjustments would in turn systematically inform the next year's cycle of the iterated planning process.

Robin concludes the discussion of incorrect criticisms of his planning model by saying that this really has nothing to do with an articulation of planning and market processes: "But none of this has anything to do with how to come up with a comprehensive economic plan in the first place—which was the problem we tackled initially." He could be right about this if the adjustments are small to the comprehensive plan that comes out of the iterated participatory planning process. The initial plan, after all, will include some number of size 6½, purple women's high-heeled, leatherless shoes with a yellow toe, and perhaps this is pretty close to what people will actually want when they actually buy shoes. But if the adjustments are large, and if they require significant shifting around of actual allocations of resources, then these supply and demand feedback processes and adjustments which "look like a market and smell like a market" will have much more the character of actual market processes. In effect this means that the planning process itself is not in fact *comprehensive*, but rather loosely constructed. It is a hybrid of planning and market processes, not a pure form of either. I see no problem with this because I do not see this as inherently generating pernicious antisocial effects.

4. Mathematical Models of Complex Systems

One of the interesting issues that has run through our dialogue is the contrast between the methods by which Robin and I envision alternatives. Robin has developed an elaborate model of a future possible economic system. At its core this involves formal mathematical models in which various kinds of consistent outcomes can be demonstrated, given the assumptions of the model, including behavioral assumptions about agents. While these formal models have not directly figured in our exchanges in this dialogue, they have been periodically referred to in footnotes, and in any case constitute the foundation for Robin's belief that his proposed procedures of iterated participatory planning will produce consistent prices that fully embody the social costs of production and an allocation of resources needed to produce the planned output. My approach has been to elaborate the normative principles we would want to see embodied in ideal economic institutions and then explore a wide variety of quite different institutional forms that could help realize those values without positing a model of an overarching unified system within which these diverse institutional arrangements would fit together and function seamlessly.

While Robin supports many of the specific proposals I endorse in my account of socialism and real utopias, nevertheless he argues that my pluralist approach has significant limitations:

> I hope it is clear by now that I not only regard "institutional pluralism *in transition*," including markets, as a practical necessity, but also appreciate that pluralism in transition provides a valuable way to test different ideas about how best to organize economic activities. However, in my opinion "institutional pluralism of the destination" can be an excuse for imprecise reasoning, which fails to follow assumptions through to their logical conclusions . . . While Erik no longer misinterprets the model of a participatory economy as a strategic transitional program, I think he still underestimates the usefulness of elaborating rigorous models of future economic systems.

Let me try to clarify my view of "rigorous models of future economic systems," especially the kind of comprehensive models elaborated by Robin.

I absolutely agree that it is useful to develop formal mathematical models and deploy them within discussions of social transformation. They clarify the logic of ideas and the implications of different design features. They alert us to potential problems. They are a critical part of the intellectual map of envisioning alternatives. Just as I advocate viewing economic systems as ecosystems combining qualitatively different forms of economic organization, so I think the optimal intellectual ecosystem for emancipatory theory should contain a wide variety of different forms of theoretical and empirical work.

But I also believe that too much reliance on formal models can create overconfidence that the complexities and dynamics of the actual world do not seriously undermine the predicted smoothness of the model. There is a tendency for people who are really good at constructing formal mathematical models of social processes to treat real-world complexity as disturbances and noise, rather than as problems that could potentially severely undermine the expected outcomes.

If it should come to pass that someday people are in a position to institute an emancipatory economic system along the lines of participatory planning, I don't know what the problems will be and whether they will be just minor wrinkles that require practical implementation adjustments, or whether they will involve more fundamental issues. I suspect that it is not even possible to know how system complexity will shape the optimal way of navigating whatever problems occur.

Robin acknowledges that there will be lots of experimentation and modification of the ideas he proposes in his model. He does not claim that the specific details of his iterated planning process with a facilitation board and various kinds of councils constitute a full-blown blueprint for an alternative economy. The specific design of these institutions will emerge out of an extended process of democratic experimentalism. But he is quite confident—and I feel over-confident—that there will be no necessity for markets in the institutional configuration of a democratic, egalitarian, cooperative economy. I think he believes this because his equations show that markets are not needed. It is on this strong confidence in the conclusions derived from formal models that we disagree.

The upshot of these arguments is that in the intellectual ecosystem of emancipatory thinking it is certainly desirable to have some people pushing ideas anchored in models of a unitary system-building totality. But we also need institutional pluralists who attempt to give precision to the idea of a heterogeneous loosely coupled system embodying emancipatory values.

5. The Ultimate Need for System-Rupture

As in many of the themes in our dialogue, Robin and I have similar views about many aspects of the process of transformation. In particular, we share a strong commitment to struggles for progressive reforms, both because these can make life better for people and because they can help pave the road for more radical transformation in the future. He also endorses the importance of what I call interstitial and symbiotic strategies and transformations as a way of thinking about such reform processes.

Where we may differ is in the question of whether or not at some point in the future a system-level rupture might be needed, and if needed, would be actually possible. Commenting on my account of situations in which sharp confrontations with capitalist elites may be necessary, Robin poses the problem this way:

> I am disappointed with Erik's formulation of how we should behave when such situations arise: "The purpose of such confrontations, however, is not a systemic rupture with capitalist dominance, but rather creating more space for the interplay of interstitial and symbiotic strategies." At some point "creating more space for interplay" must give way to "a systemic rupture with capitalist dominance," which means abolishing the institutional basis for their dominance, the private enterprise market system. When decisive moments come one either defeats an enemy and disarms him to prevent war from erupting anew, or one fails to do so. In moments of confrontation unfortunately, in my opinion, those with a personal inclination toward symbiotic and interstitial strategies are all too likely to make the same mistake Swedish social democrats made in 1975. At moments when those who hesitate are lost, leadership with more "ruptural inclinations" becomes more socially useful. Why, when we get the chance, should we hesitate to drive our stake through the vampire's heart?

This is a potent argument, for unquestionably there are situations in which progressive reform is completely blocked. Robin is correct when he writes, "Incrementalism also has no answers for situations where one must either make a qualitative change or accept eventual re-stabilization back to the old status quo." But, of course, it does not follow that simply because incrementalism has no answer for this problem, system-ruptures are actually possible, that they could succeed in their stated objective of "*abolishing* the institutional basis for [capitalist] dominance." System-ruptural strategies may be wishful thinking rather than genuine answers to the question "what is to be done?" in these situations. It is one thing to argue that in the case of political dictatorships a seizure of power could be capable of transforming the institutions of the state in a democratic way, and quite another to say that a seizure of power can successfully both abolish something as complex as capitalism *and replace it with a participatory democratic alternative*. I do not have an answer to the problem of what should be done in the face of the impossibility of further incremental advance, but I remain skeptical that a systemic rupture in which capitalism is effectively abolished could result in an emancipatory alternative.

When thinking about the foundational transformation of core power relations within an economic system, the metaphor of "driving the stake through the vampire's heart" is gravely misleading. The metaphor suggests that there is a single center of agency and power that can be decisively destroyed and whose destruction effectively removes the main obstacle to transformation. This is, of course, the way revolutionaries have often thought about social revolution: seize state power, destroy the enemy, and clear the way for building a new society "on the ashes of the old." Robin and I both regard this as an unrealistic strategy for the United States today, but is it likely ever to be a plausible strategy for the purposes creating a radically egalitarian democratic economy and society? The historical evidence weighs against this possibility: revolutionary ruptures have been capable of transforming state power, and they have also, in a few notable instances, been capable of abolishing the core class relations of existing economic systems, but so far they have not shown any capacity to build even the rudiments of democratic-egalitarian, emancipatory alternatives.

Robin invokes the case of Sweden in 1975 when the Social Democrats initially proposed, and then in the face of strong opposition from Swedish capital, backed away from a proposal to gradually democratize ownership of large Swedish corporations through the use of a novel kind of wage-earner fund. Robin uses a military image to set up his reference to the Swedish situation: "When decisive moments come one either defeats an enemy and disarms him to prevent war from erupting anew, or one fails to do so." This just does not seem an apt way of thinking about the foundational transformation of capitalism in Sweden. While I agree with him that it is conceivable that Swedish Social Democracy might have been able to enact their wage-earner funds plan if they had been willing to confront capital head on, it seems implausible that they would have been able to abolish "the institutional basis for [capitalist] dominance, the private enterprise market system." The most that could have been hoped for would have been a shift in the power relations within the "economic ecosystem" in which capitalism would have been rendered less dominant and perhaps even subordinate to more democratically organized economic relations.

There are, then, two fundamental issues a ruptural argument must confront: first, under what condition would it be possible to really "abolish" something as complex as "the institutional basis of capitalism," and second, under what conditions would that abolition actually result in a democratic-egalitarian alternative. We know from historical experience that it is possible to destroy the private enterprise market system without creating a democratic-egalitarian alternative. What is unclear is whether—under other conditions not yet historically encountered—a ruptural, abolitionist attack on capitalism could have genuinely emancipatory results.

The only condition in which I think a successful systemic rupture might actually lead to an emancipatory alternative is one in which it was the case that the hybrid economic ecosystem had already shifted to one in which participatory, democratic-egalitarian economic relations had become the core of the economy.[6] If over an extended period of time interstitial and symbiotic strategies had transformed the economy in this way, then the institution-building tasks following a rupture would be fairly modest and the chaotic processes unleashed by rupture perhaps manageable. This scenario, however, seems to be ruled out by Robin's skepticism that anti-capitalist, egalitarian, and cooperative economic processes could ever reach such a threshold so long as capitalism remains a powerful component of the economic system. We are therefore left with the conclusion that (1) a successful rupture with capitalism in which the private enterprise market system is abolished and a participatory economy is established is only possible if a participatory economy has already reached near dominance within the economic ecosystem, but (2) a participatory economy cannot reach that level of development so long as capitalism is dominant. It therefore may well be true that incrementalism does not have an answer to the problem of overcoming absolute barriers to transformation. Unfortunately, the same is true for ruptural strategies:

---

6 This is—roughly—the way capitalism replaced feudalism: proto-capitalist economic processes had already become the dynamic core of the economy at the time that feudal centers of power were effectively abolished.

they have no answer to the problem of actually advancing a democratic egalitarian economy and society in the aftermath of a rupture.

Conclusion

Where, then, does this leave us?

A critical issue for a political project of emancipatory transformation is having an array of practical, achievable objectives that make life better for people in the world as it is and are connected to the vision for a fundamentally different kind of economy and society. Having a strategic scenario that can take us all the way from here to there matters much less. On the core strategic issues, Robin and I are largely in agreement. Both of us argue that another world is possible in which people have vastly more equal access to the conditions to live flourishing lives than they do in capitalism and vastly greater capacity to directly shape the conditions of their own lives through an array of empowered participatory processes. We also both believe that much can be done now to mitigate the damage to people's lives created by the dominance of capitalism, and that some of the things we can do also prefigure this alternative world.

Still, there are some real differences in our views—on the potential role for markets within the structural configurations of the desired destination, on the level of our confidence that we can actually anticipate the kinds of dilemmas and trade-offs that will exist even in the ideal world we want, and, perhaps, on the necessity at some point for a systemic rupture. These differences, however, may in the end have almost no practical implications. I suspect that the time horizon before the issue of attempting a systemic rupture with capitalism in developed capitalist countries is very far in the future, and that it is even further in the future before the issue of whether or not markets should be abolished will be on the political agenda of any democratic society. But I also doubt that one's beliefs now about what should be decided under those future conditions would greatly affect any choices about strategies and initiatives today. It is in this sense that I think the main thing is to be very clear about fundamental values and the critique of capitalism, about the possibility of realizing those values to a much greater extent in alternative economic institutions, and about the practical initiatives we can undertake today that move us in that direction.

Acknowledgements

Robin would like to thank Mesa Refuge, a writers' retreat in Point Reyes Station, California, where he was a resident for two weeks during this last year.

About the Authors

Robin Hahnel is Professor Emeritus from American University in Washington DC where he taught in the department of economics for thirty-three years. He has also taught as a visiting professor at the Catholic University in Lima, Peru; the University of Manchester in Manchester, England; and most recently at Lewis and Clark College and Portland State University in Portland, Oregon. He has been active in left politics for over forty-five years, beginning with New Left SDS chapters at Harvard and MIT in the 1960s, and most recently with Economics for Equity and the Environment and Jobs with Justice in Portland, Oregon.

He is best known as co-creator, together with Michael Albert, of the alternative to capitalism known as "participatory economics" (*The Political Economy of Participatory Economics* [New Jersey and Oxford: Princeton University Press, 1991]). His most recent books are *Economic Justice and Democracy: From Competition to Cooperation* (New York and Oxon: Routledge, 2005); *Green Economics: Confronting the Ecological Crisis* (New York: M. E. Sharpe, 2011); *Of the People, By the People: The Case for a Participatory Economy* (Oakland: AK Press, 2012); and *The ABCs of Political Economy: A Modern Approach*, 2nd edition (London: Pluto Books, 2014).

Erik Olin Wright has taught sociology at the University of Wisconsin since 1976 where he is currently Vilas Distinguished Professor of Sociology. His academic work has been centrally concerned with reconstructing the Marxist tradition of social theory and research in ways that attempt to make it more relevant to contemporary concerns and more cogent as a scientific framework of analysis. His empirical research has focused especially on the changing character of class relations in developed capitalist societies. Since 1992 he has directed the *Real Utopias Project* series, which explores a wide range of proposals for new institutional designs that embody emancipatory ideals and yet are attentive to issues of pragmatic feasibility. He was president of the American Sociological Association in 2011–12.

His principal publications include: *The Politics of Punishment* (Harper Collins, 1973); *Classes* (London and New York: Verso, 1985); *The Debate on Classes* (London and New York: Verso, 1990); *Interrogating Inequality* (London and New York: Verso, 1994); *Class Counts: Comparative Studies in Class Analysis* (Cambridge: Cambridge University Press, 1997); *Envisioning Real Utopias* (London and New York: Verso, 2010); with Archon Fung, *Deepening Democracy: Institutional Innovations in Empowered Participatory Governance* (London and New York: Verso, 2003); and with Joel Rogers, *American Society: How It Really Works* (London: W.W. Norton, 2011). He is also the editor of the *Real Utopias Project* series, published by Verso Books. His forthcoming book, *Understanding Class* (London and New York: Verso, 2015), proposes a framework for integrating the insights of different traditions of class analysis. He is currently working on a new manuscript, *Sociological Marxism* (London and New York: Verso, tentatively, 2017).

Website: ssc.wisc.edu/~wright

Printed in the United States
By Bookmasters